George Lopez

Other books in the People in the News series:

Maya Angelou	Coretta Scott King
Tyra Banks	Ashton Kutcher
David Beckham	Tobey Maguire
Beyoncé	Eli Manning
Fidel Castro	John McCain
Kelly Clarkson	Barack Obama
Hillary Clinton	Michelle Obama
Miley Cyrus	Danica Patrick
Ellen Degeneres	Nancy Pelosi
Hilary Duff	Queen Latifah
Zac Efron	Daniel Radcliffe
Brett Favre	Condoleezza Rice
50 Cent	Rihanna
Al Gore	J.K. Rowling
Tony Hawk	Shakira
Salma Hayek	Tupac Shakur
LeBron James	Will Smith
Jay-Z	Gwen Stefani
Derek Jeter	Ben Stiller
Steve Jobs	Hilary Swank
Dwayne Johnson	Justin Timberlake
Angelina Jolie	Usher
Jonas Brothers	Denzel Washington
Kim Jong II	Oprah Winfrey

George Lopez

by Terri Dougherty

LUCENT BOOKS
A part of Gale, Cengage Learning

GALE
CENGAGE Learning

Detroit • New York • San Francisco • New Haven, Conn • Waterville, Maine • London

LIBRARY OF CONGRESS CATALOGING-IN-PUBLICATION DATA

Dougherty, Terri.
  George Lopez / by Terri Dougherty.
    p. cm. -- (People in the news)
  Includes bibliographical references and index.
  ISBN 978-1-4205-0424-8
  1. Lopez, George, 1961-2. Comedians--United States--Biography. 3. Television actors
and actresses--United States--Biography. I. Title.
  PN2287.L633D68 2011
  792.7'6028092--dc22
  [B]
                                           2010047341

Lucent Books
27500 Drake Rd
Farmington Hills MI 48331

ISBN-13: 978-1-4205-0424-8
ISBN-10: 1-4205-0424-X

Printed in the United States of America
1 2 3 4 5 6 7 15 14 13 12 11

Printed by Bang Printing, Brainerd, MN, 1st Ptg., 03/2011

Contents

ame and celebrity are alluring. People are drawn to those who walk in fame's spotlight, whether they are known for great accomplishments or for notorious deeds. The lives of the famous pique public interest and attract attention, perhaps because their experiences seem in some ways so different from, yet in other ways so similar to, our own.

Newspapers, magazines, and television regularly capitalize on this fascination with celebrity by running profiles of famous people. For example, television programs such as *Entertainment Tonight* devote all their programming to stories about entertainment and entertainers. Magazines such as *People* fill their pages with stories of the private lives of famous people. Even newspapers, newsmagazines, and television news frequently delve into the lives of well-known personalities. Despite the number of articles and programs, few provide more than a superficial glimpse at their subjects.

Lucent's People in the News series offers young readers a deeper look into the lives of today's newsmakers, the influences that have shaped them, and the impact they have had in their fields of endeavor and on other people's lives. The subjects of the series hail from many disciplines and walks of life. They include authors, musicians, athletes, political leaders, entertainers, entrepreneurs, and others who have made a mark on modern life and who, in many cases, will continue to do so for years to come.

These biographies are more than factual chronicles. Each book emphasizes the contributions, accomplishments, or deeds that have brought fame or notoriety to the individual and shows how that person has influenced modern life. Authors portray their subjects in a realistic, unsentimental light. For example, Bill Gates—the cofounder and chief executive officer of the software giant Microsoft—has been instrumental in making personal computers the most vital tool of the modern age. Few dispute his business savvy, his perseverance, or his technical expertise, yet critics say he is ruthless in his dealings with competitors and driven more by his desire to maintain Microsoft's dominance in the computer industry than by an interest in furthering technology.

In these books, young readers will encounter inspiring stories about real people who achieved success despite enormous obstacles. Oprah Winfrey—the most powerful, most watched, and wealthiest woman on television today—spent the first six years of her life in the care of her grandparents while her unwed mother sought work and a better life elsewhere. Her adolescence was colored by pregnancy at age fourteen, rape, and sexual abuse.

Each author documents and supports his or her work with an array of primary and secondary source quotations taken from diaries, letters, speeches, and interviews. All quotes are footnoted to show readers exactly how and where biographers derive their information and provide guidance for further research. The quotations enliven the text by giving readers eyewitness views of the life and accomplishments of each person covered in the People in the News series.

In addition, each book in the series includes photographs, annotated bibliographies, timelines, and comprehensive indexes. For both the casual reader and the student researcher, the People in the News series offers insight into the lives of today's newsmakers—people who shape the way we live, work, and play in the modern age.

Laughing Through Pain

One of the first episodes of the television sitcom *George Lopez* deals with the lead character George's dislike of birthdays. He cannot believe that parents spoil their children with parties and bring them to kid-centered restaurants such as Chuck E. Cheese. If he had wanted to go to the restaurant with the mouse mascot, his mother would have told him to look behind the refrigerator. "There were about five Chuckies running around back there,"[1] he says.

Being denied a birthday party is a miserable experience for a child, but it is this type of painful personal experience that has fueled Lopez's success in comedy. His difficult upbringing formed the basis for a comedy act and television show that gained widespread viewership in syndication. Lopez's wry observations about his Hispanic background and the American lifestyle have generated laughs and catapulted him to stardom.

Laughter from Tears

Lopez readily draws upon his Mexican American heritage for jokes, yet reaches audiences with an emotional brand of comedy that crosses cultural boundaries. People love to laugh at the brutally honest stories of others, and Lopez has had plenty of heartache to share. He was abandoned by both parents and raised by a grandmother who did not show her love for or pride in her grandson.

She thought she had to make George tough by withholding affection. She did not want him to expect happiness, so she treated him harshly to get him used to rejection and disappointment.

His grandmother's mean streak eventually struck Lopez as funny, but it took years for him to be able to base material on his painful childhood memories. Once he did, he discovered a deep, unique sense of humor that set him apart as a performer.

Overcoming unhappy memories was just one obstacle Lopez faced as he built his career. He also had a negative, angry attitude that made it difficult for him to rebound when his career faltered. Lopez initially went down several dead-end paths. When he was a young man, Lopez dealt with setbacks by quitting. As a struggling comic, he got angry when his career did not take off quickly. He drank too much to dull the pain of a dismal performance. Until he learned to face setbacks constructively, he could not take his career where he dreamed it could go.

Another issue Lopez had to confront was how Hispanics were viewed in the entertainment industry. He was initially labeled a Latino comedian, which, he felt, gave him no opportunity to play larger venues because of the assumption in the entertainment industry that a Latino comedian could not appeal to a broad, mainstream American audience. He also did not like the acting roles he was offered because they perpetuated negative Hispanic stereotypes. He shied away from movies and television shows that would have cast him as a gang member or drug dealer, but then felt he was being held back professionally because of his ethnicity. Self-pity, anger, and depression overwhelmed him.

A New Outlook

Lopez's career did not take off until Lopez changed his attitude and approach. While he was unable to change others' biases and stereotypes directly, he learned to change the way he reacted to these obstacles. Lopez created an act that was personal and touching, one that helped audiences connect with him and indirectly helped change public attitudes. He began including jokes that had roots in his painful childhood. For example, he joked

George Lopez, appearing at the unveiling of his star on the Hollywood Walk of Fame in 2006, overcame an uphappy childhood to become a successful comedian whose material draws upon aspects of Hispanic culture.

about his grandfather trying to assemble a bike for him while drunk. He wrote a comedy bit about his grandmother never saying sorry, even when she hit him with the car. He imitated the way Mexican and white Americans spoke and saw things differently. He got into character rather than simply delivering observations. His revised act eventually caught the eye of influential people who got him on national network television. He took that once-in-a-lifetime opportunity to prove that his brand of humor had a place in mainstream America.

Lopez's humor is at times controversial, as he is not afraid to talk about stereotypes, personal issues, or race in his act. Some think that his material is too hard on Hispanics, others that it places too much emphasis on Hispanics' importance in American society. Lopez admits to both emphases. His humor does sometimes focus on negative aspects of Hispanic culture, yet he does not shy away from encouraging Hispanic pride. He does not hesitate to speak Spanish in his stand-up act or poke fun at both

Anglo and Hispanic cultures. People need to laugh at themselves, he believes, and getting an audience to laugh has always been his goal.

America's Entertainer

Lopez has successfully navigated close to the line of going too far without crossing it, and as a result has become a popular mainstream comedian. He broke new ground in television with *George Lopez,* the first successful series with a Latino cast. In 2009 he became the first Hispanic late-night talk show host with *Lopez Tonight.* He plays to large crowds as a stand-up performer, and his popularity crosses cultural boundaries.

Lopez wants his career to inspire others. As a child, Lopez had few role models to guide him; as an adult, he wants to be the role model he never had. He wants to show that Hispanics can make it in the entertainment industry and in any other field they put their mind to. Hispanics ought "to be included in the fabric of America," he has said. "We're part of it."[2] He also wants to show all Americans that dreams can be achieved without a support- ive or privileged background, and that the things that are most painful in life can become a foundation for accomplishment and happiness. "I've made quite a life for myself just with the ability to write on a blank piece of paper,"[3] he says, and he hopes his phenomenal and at times unlikely success will help others muster the courage to do the same.

Growing Pains

Geroge Lopez is known for making people laugh, but the first years of his life were anything but funny. He grew up in Southern California in a home where love and kindness were rarely shown. The grandmother who raised him thought it was better to make him tough than show him affection, and she communicated with sarcasm and harsh words.

To cope with a difficult life at home, George developed a sharp sense of humor. This grew into an interest in comedy and led to dreams of a career as a comedian. Before he could make a life out of making people laugh, however, George first had to endure his share of heartache.

Abandoned by His Mother

George Lopez was born on April 23, 1961 in East Los Angeles, California. His parents brought him into the world but had little to do with his upbringing. His father, whom George recalled had the unusual name of Anatasio, only stayed around for the first few months of his life. Anatasio was a migrant worker from Mexico who abandoned George when he was two months old. George was left in the care of his Mexican American mother, Frieda, who was twenty years old and unprepared to raise a child. She had not finished high school and could not read or write, and so had difficulty earning enough money to support herself and her son. She had trouble holding down a job, and she had a reputation for not paying her bills. George recalls that when the ice cream man passed by, rather than asking what

Storefronts in a section of East Los Angeles in the 1960s display Spanish-language signs because its population was largely of Mexican descent. Lopez was born in East Los Angeles in 1961.

flavor the boy wanted, he would tell George that Frieda owed him money.

George's mother's friends were rough characters with questionable morals. George once awoke to his mother dancing on the kitchen table in front of a crowd of rowdy friends. Because of his mother's unstable lifestyle, George found little happiness at home, and by the time he was four George spent a lot of time in the care of his grandmother, Frieda's mother. "Hard as I try, I can't conjure up a single pleasant thought or happy memory of my mom,"[4] he wrote in his autobiography.

George's mother also had medical problems that were difficult for George to understand as a child. She suffered from epilepsy, a disease that causes people to have seizures, violent fits that make them lose control of their body. Frieda would sometimes suffer a seizure in front of her young son. He could only call for help, and then wait for the seizure to end. Also disturbing to George were his mother's emotional problems. She once attempted to kill herself and was subsequently placed in a mental institution. During her hospitalization, George lived with his grandmother but visited his mother on Sundays. Visiting her was often scary, as he usually found Frieda heavily sedated and emotionless.

George's life remained unsettled even after his mother was released from the mental institution. He was again shuttled between his mother's and his grandmother's houses. When George was ten, Frieda began dating an older man and eventually moved to Northern California with him. After they married, she left George permanently in the care of his grandmother and had little contact with him.

"Without Hope," California

After his mother remarried, George lived full-time with his maternal grandmother, Benita Gutierrez, and her husband, Refugio. They had a small home in Mission Hills, California, a northern suburb of Los Angeles in the San Fernando Valley. His grandmother had lived in the house since the early 1960s and had raised six children there.

The small house was on a run-down street bordered by a laundromat and a highway. Lopez saw little hope for a better life when he looked around his neighborhood. The Mexican immigrants who lived there had come to America hoping for success, but had found little to welcome them and had made little progress in achieving their dreams. Many of the men found jobs in construction, working for a few weeks or a month at a time. "Our little corner of the Valley could have been named Without Hope," Lopez says. "Mexicans weren't even a class of people in Southern California. Nobody amounted to much of anything where I lived. High school was a pipe dream. Nobody worked with their head. Nobody saved. Nobody stood up for themselves."[5]

Lopez holds a copy of his autobiography, "Why You Crying?", in which he reveals details of his difficult upbringing.

The bleak neighborhood atmosphere was not the only dispiriting thing about George's childhood. The home he shared with his grandmother and step-grandfather lacked warmth and affection. Although they provided him with food and a place to live, Benita and Refugio offered little emotional support. His family did not value bonding or being together. After school, no one asked him how his day went. If he was watching a television show in one room and others were watching it in another, no one thought to ask him to join them. His grandmother never celebrated his birthday and did not bother to take pictures of him as he grew up. She disciplined him harshly. If George cried after she hit him, she would ask why he was crying, and threaten to hit him harder.

The First High School Graduate

School was not highly valued by some of Lopez's family members, who regarded educated people as snobby or arrogant. However, George's step-grandfather, Refugio Gutierrez, strongly encouraged him to finish high school. In 1979, he became the first person in his extended family to graduate from high school. He walked across the stage in a cap and gown like the other students in his class, but received his actual diploma a few months after the ceremony. He needed to make up a credit in English over the summer, but once that class was finished he was proud to call himself a high school graduate.

A Loveless Family

His family also ruthlessly made fun of him, even when he needed medical care. For example, he wet the bed as a child, the result of an undiagnosed kidney disorder. His family did not know that a physical condition was making him wet the bed, and did not take him to the doctor to find out why it happened. Instead, "they'd yell at me," he recalled years later. "Nobody tried to figure out why I did it."[6]

Not until he was an adult did George realize that his grandmother's behavior and attitude stemmed from how she herself had been raised as a child. She did not celebrate his birthday, for example, because she had never had a birthday party herself. "I didn't know what birthdays were,"[7] she told a *New York Times* interviewer. In fact, George's grandmother had a similarly harsh childhood. She was raised by an aunt in a California farming community after her mother was deported to Mexico. She was shown little appreciation or love by her family, and was made to cook and clean for them until she ran away at age sixteen.

Lopez throws out a ceremonial first pitch at a Los Angeles Dodgers game in 2009. One of his better childhood memories is of attending Dodgers games with his step-grandfather.

She married a man who beat her, and had raised six difficult children by him. She eventually divorced her abusive husband and married Refugio, whom George considers the most influential man in his life.

George got along better with Refugio than he did with his grandmother. A mutual love of baseball helped forge a connection between the two. They talked naturally and easily about the sport, and outings to see the Los Angeles Dodgers play at Dodger Stadium were the closest thing to a comfortable family relationship that George had. "We ate together, which we never did at home, and we had a common interest,"[8] George recalled.

George's relationship with his step-grandfather was far from warm and caring, however. For example, George played baseball on a Little League team, but Refugio rarely came to see him play. He did not congratulate him when he did well or tell George he was proud of him. In addition, the older man's drinking strained their relationship. When Refugio drank too much, he became mean. He would argue with George and hit him on the side of his head. "I don't want to sound like I'm auditioning for Oprah or anything, but I don't think there was ever a moment in my childhood when I felt it was great to be part of a family," he writes in his autobiography. "Not a single one. It was awful not to have money, happiness, warmth, love, attention, or affection. Just awful."[9]

Coping Through Comedy

His grandparents' inability to show love for him, Refugio's alcoholic outbursts, and his dismal neighborhood gave George little to enjoy as a child. He used humor to cope with his loneliness and unhappiness. Often, he made jokes at his own expense, which was easy for him to do because he thought poorly of himself. He was especially uncomfortable with his looks: he thought he was fat, his head too big and his lips too large. His low self-image was reinforced by the taunts of other children, who called him Spuds because his head and features were large and rounded.

Latino comedian Freddie Prinze became a role model for Lopez when he decided to pursue comedy as a young teen.

George often took refuge in television. When he immersed himself in a children's program, comedy, or talk show, he forgot for a while the pain and difficulty of his own life. He enjoyed coming home to an empty house after school and turning on the TV—it helped push away the loneliness and emptiness he felt.

Freddie Prinze

Freddie Prinze was both Puerto Rican and Hungarian, and often referred to himself as "Hunga Rican." After a successful late-night television appearance on *The Tonight Show* with Johnny Carson in 1973, Prinze won his own television series, *Chico and the Man*, which first aired in 1974. It starred Prinze as a Chicano who lived in East Los Angeles and worked at a garage with a grumpy owner, played by Jack Albertson. *Chico and the Man* was the first American television series ever to be set in a Mexican American neighborhood, and Prinze achieved rare mainstream success as a Hispanic performer. Prinze had a promising career ahead of himself when he committed suicide in 1977, at the age of twenty-two.

His love of television and his ability to make people laugh gave George a career goal at an unusually young age. By the time he was eleven, George was determined to be a comedian. By age thirteen, he had a comic role model to follow. He saw a televised performance by Latino comedian Freddie Prinze Sr. and was captivated. George not only appreciated Prinze's humor and comic timing, but also enjoyed watching a comedian who looked like him. All of the adults he knew worked in factories or were laborers. For the first time, he saw someone with a Latino background making a living making people laugh.

A Struggle to Get Through High School

George's interest in comedy grew as a student at San Fernando High School, where it both helped and hurt him. He was an average student who could make his classmates laugh but also had a

A Young Golfer

George discovered his love of the game of golf when he was around twelve years old. He would often amuse himself by practicing hitting lemons and limes toward the gas station across the street from his backyard. He did not get to work on the finer points of the game, however: His family owned just two golf clubs, which were used mainly to prop open a door or to scare away a burglar. Lopez began playing more seriously in his twenties and formally learned the game at a public course in the Sylmar district of Los Angeles.

Mexican American golfer Lee Trevino, left, poses with Lopez at Pebble Beach in 2006. Lopez was inspired as a boy to take up the game after watching Trevino play.

Though golf is traditionally regarded as an upper-class, white person's sport, Lopez was inspired to play by famed professional golfer Lee Trevino. Trevino, who is Mexican American, had also grown up poor and had been abandoned by his father. Trevino helped Lopez view golf as a sport that he could play regardless of his ethnic background or economic status. "To be Mexican-American at a time when our culture was really invisible, and to slay the best golfers in the world with a homemade, 'freehand' swing—which is such a Mexican thing—and for me to see that with the big eyes of a kid, as a lot of young kids connect success to Tiger [Woods], I connect my success to Lee," Lopez says.

Quoted in Jamie Diaz, "G-Lo," *Golf Digest*, February 2008, p. 104.

tendency to use comedy to disrupt the class and gain attention. He also developed a questionable reputation, thanks to a drug bust when he was a freshman. His cousin gave him a bag of marijuana to keep in his locker. When the principal found it, George was arrested and taken to the police station. After the incident, George's grandmother sent him to live with an uncle near San Diego for a month. Despite this episode, George claims he did not use drugs or drink while he was in high school. He says he preferred going places with friends or playing games with the kids in the neighborhood.

Although George could frequently break up class with a joke, he never fully felt like he fit in in high school. He showed little interest in clubs or team sports. He played baseball, but quit the team during his senior year after being benched. He remembers himself as neither cool nor popular, but rather as a student who was present but not really involved.

George also received little support from his teachers. When he told his drama teacher of his hope for a career in comedy, for example, the teacher belittled him. Although the teacher did stand-up comedy himself, he said he did not have time to teach the finer points of the craft to his student.

Determined to Make It

George found his own comedy mentors during his high school years. He loved watching the stand-up routines of professional comedians, especially Richard Pryor. Pryor was an edgy comedian with a volatile personality. His energetic performances, peppered with foul language and bold racial material, provided outlandish entertainment for appreciative crowds. After watching Pryor's Long Beach concert on television in 1979, George became mesmerized by his style and ability.

Although he gained inspiration from Pryor while in high school, George also lost a great role model while he was a teen. George was crushed when the troubled Freddie Prinze killed himself in 1977 after battling drug addiction and personal issues. George was stunned by the news, but did not stop admiring

Richard Pryor, a popular but edgy stand-up comedian and actor, was one of Lopez's idols.

Prinze, who taught him it was possible for someone of Latino heritage to become a successful comedian. He continued to watch and learn from stand-up comedians, particularly those who broke racial barriers to achieve success. Comedy represented the only glimmer of happiness in George's difficult life, and he was determined to make it as a comedian.

Chapter 2

Comic Commitment

The only career Lopez ever considered was that of stand-up comedian, and he did not wait long to begin pursuing his dream. On the day he finished high school, Lopez took the stage for the first time. On June 4, 1979, Lopez walked through the graduation ceremony at San Fernando High School. That evening he appeared onstage during "open mic night" at a comedy club in the Los Angeles area. Lopez knew he could be funny, but he found that making a joke with a group of friends or in a classroom was very different from making jokes before a room full of strangers.

A Rocky Start

Open mic nights offer amateur comedians the chance to get onstage and try out their material on a live audience. Would-be comics are not paid for their act, but the experience is invaluable just the same. It is a chance to get over stage fright, learn to improvise and deal with hecklers, get to know other talented comedians, and maybe impress a scout in the audience. With the help of his friend Ernie Arellano, Lopez generated material and carefully planned his routine in anticipation of his first open mic night.

Once onstage, however, Lopez realized that having something funny to say is only part of what makes a comedian successful. Delivery and self-confidence count too, but Lopez had neither

An empty comedy club awaits performers and an audience. Lopez made his first appearance at a comedy club the night of his high school graduation in 1979.

of these. He was so nervous in front of the crowd that he lost all sense of comic timing. Once he started talking, he could not stop. He chaotically delivered a rapid series of jokes on topics such as Mexicans and fake accents. The audience had no time to digest his material, and the only time anyone laughed was when he finally paused to take a breath. It was a terrible debut. "The first night was awful because I was so afraid," he recalled. "My hands were sweaty and I couldn't swallow."[10] Lopez quickly realized that stand-up comedy was more than just telling jokes and soaking in applause.

He was not discouraged, though, and worked to improve his stage presence. He and Ernie continued to write new material. George practiced his delivery until his timing improved. By his third performance, everything clicked. He improvised his first joke, making fun of the comedian who had just performed. The audience loved it. Getting others to laugh and hearing their applause sent him reeling with confidence.

Ernie had a cassette tape recorder and recorded Lopez's act that night. Right after his performance, they dashed out of the

The Improv on Melrose

The Improv on Melrose, where Arsenio Hall saw George Lopez perform, is a popular comedy club in Los Angeles, California. The club was opened in 1975 as an offshoot of a New York–based club that was initially called Improvisation. The New York club was founded in the early 1960s as a place for actors to meet and enjoy sing-alongs, but its focus soon switched to comedy.

The California club received nationwide exposure in the 1980s and 1990s through the cable series *An Evening at the Improv*. The show featured stand-up acts by such comedians as Andy Kaufman, Jim Carrey, and Tim Allen.

The Improv on Melrose continues to be a place where aspiring comedians try to get noticed, but it is not the only Improv offering stand-up comedy. In addition to the New York and Los Angeles locations, there are Improv comedy clubs in Arlington, Texas; Chicago, Illinois; Pittsburgh, Pennsylvania; and more than a dozen other cities.

club and down the street, looking for someplace quiet where they could listen to the tape. Hearing the audience's enthusiastic response again energized George. "It was the first time in my life that I felt loved and accepted ... and it was by complete strangers," he said. "Once I got that in me, I chased that high forever."[11] Lopez experienced a feeling of acceptance from a group of strangers that he had never felt even from his own family.

As he basked in the afterglow of the crowd's approval, everything sad, frustrating, and disappointing about his life briefly disappeared. Lopez felt great about himself, and it was a feeling he wanted to experience again and again. His taste of success made him all the more determined to become a professional comedian. As he wrote on a slip of paper on August 6, 1979: "I know at times I can't make it but eventually I will. And I will hit the American people like a hammer. I will be the best."[12]

Doubt Creeps In

Soon after Lopez's initial success, however, he hit an unexpected emotional wall. His routines received mixed results—sometimes he got laughs, but other times his jokes flopped. He began to realize that stand-up comedy was an emotionally taxing endeavor. It was hard not to take it personally when an audience heckled him or, even worse, met his act with silence. Gradually, the fear of rejection overshadowed his confidence. It became increasingly difficult for Lopez to summon the courage to go onstage. He became less and less sure of himself and sometimes would not bother to perform at all. He continued to sign up at open mic night, but about half of the time he would leave before his name was called.

Over the next six months, Lopez wondered if his personality was a good fit for stand-up comedy. He worried he was too thin-skinned to go onstage and be judged by audiences and club managers. His self-esteem plummeted and he felt like he was constantly humiliating himself. "I was embarking on a profession where you had to be entertaining and charming, and I wasn't equipped to take it all in,"[13] he says. Finally, he decided the strain was not worth it, and left comedy in March 1980.

Without comedy, Lopez had no real goal in his late teens and early twenties. He drank and went to parties, hung out with his friend Ernie, played softball, and took jobs where he could see no future for himself. Over the next couple years, he worked at a garden supply store, shipped orders to customers at a book company, made floppy disks for computers, and tested circuit boards. Nothing lasted long, however. He left the garden supply store, was fired from the book company after he started coming in late, and lost his job at the floppy disk company. He gave education a try and enrolled in an electronics course at a trade school. However, he lasted only one night in the classroom.

The Comeback

Other kinds of work made Lopez remember that the only thing he really wanted to do was be a comedian. While working at the circuit board maker in 1982, he daydreamed about giving comedy another try. Two years had passed since he had been onstage, but now he felt ready to try again. He asked to be put on the day shift so he could visit clubs at night. He wrote new material and returned to the open mic night stage on March 1, 1982, nearly two years to the day that he had left.

This time Lopez was prepared to weather nasty comments and win over a tough audience. He understood he would have to endure bad nights if he was going to enjoy good ones. He realized that failing onstage was not so bad compared with what could go wrong at other types of jobs. "If the worst thing that can happen is that nobody laughs, then I can deal with that, because the worst thing that can happen at the factory is that I could lose a limb or be crushed by a huge machine,"[14] he says. Undaunted, Lopez tried to learn something from every performance. After each appearance he jotted down comments, observations, and ideas in a notebook he called *The Comeback*. In *The Comeback* he wrote new material, observed audiences' reactions, and made adjustments to his routine based on what worked and what did not.

A Double Life Takes Its Toll

In his early twenties, Lopez worked on polishing his act but could not make a living by comedy alone. He kept his day job, although his day job kept changing. He was laid off at the circuit board company after working there for three years. He found another job at an electronics maker, and worked there during the day to make ends meet.

But trying to build a comedy career while holding down a full-time day job was hectic. Lopez was tired after putting in a full day's work, and he filled his spare time writing rather than relaxing. Because comedy is a late-night scene, Lopez would often stay out and party with friends after his act. This cycle wore heavily on his body, and he was exhausted at work.

To keep up his double life, he began taking amphetamines to stay awake. Amphetamines are a powerful stimulant, and make a person more alert. Doctors sometimes prescribe them to people who fall asleep uncontrollably or to treat children with attention

Lopez's High Tech Jobs

Soon after high school, George Lopez took several different jobs in California's booming computer and aerospace industries. At Tandon Magnetics, Lopez made floppy disks. Floppy disks were the precursors to flash drives: they were thin, square disks that stored small amounts of data. Tandon was the first company to make a floppy disk drive for an IBM personal computer.

Lopez later got a job at a Teledyne, a California-based company that made electronic parts and instruments for the aviation industry. Lopez's job was to assemble equipment in the company's Northridge plant. In addition, Lopez worked for Sperry Aviation, a division of the giant computer electronics company, where he tested circuit boards and made sure all of the components were working properly. Lopez did not last long in any of these jobs, but gravitated toward another industry that had a significant presence in Southern California: the entertainment industry.

Lopez's character on George Lopez was a manager at an airplane parts factory, a position similar to one he held in real life while building his career as a comic.

deficit hyperactivity disorder. The drugs can be habit-forming, however, and are dangerous when taken by a person not under the care of a doctor. They can cause anxiety, depression, and violence in those who abuse them.

In his autobiography, Lopez downplays his pill habit, but it had serious repercussions for him. It became obvious to his coworkers that he was on something, and one of them eventually asked Lopez if he could get some of the same stuff he was taking. Lopez gave him a few pills, not realizing that the coworker was actually an undercover police officer. Because he was not formally dealing drugs he was not arrested, but Lopez was fired for his actions. When his grandparents found out why he had been fired, they handed out their own punishment. They were so disappointed in him that they made him move out of the house.

First Significant Gig

Getting kicked out hit Lopez hard. His grandparents had never been loving toward him, but they had always given him a roof over his head. Now he had no job and no family to help him out. He could not afford his own place, and ended up sleeping on a friend's couch. He realized that working full-time, doing stand-up comedy at night, and partying was getting him nowhere. Something had to change.

It took a few tries at more jobs that did not work out, but Lopez eventually found a more flexible position that allowed him to pursue comedy without sacrificing his health and emotional balance. Lopez got a job at an airplane parts factory in Van Nuys, California. His boss agreed to hold his job for him when he needed to take time off for comedy gigs. This let Lopez commit to paying comedy jobs that took him away for days or weeks at a time, and also gave him a steady source of income.

Lopez made his first significant comedy road trip in April 1986, at age twenty-five. He was booked at a club in Houston for a week. The club was small, but he was happy to make the trip. He was finally being paid to tell jokes. Aware that his act still needed fine-tuning, he taped each performance and studied it after each show. He did well enough to make a return trip to Houston later that year.

Making the Leap

Lopez's appearances were not yet reliable enough for him to make comedy his full-time career, however. Over the next year, he continued to work his job at the factory while he sought more paid engagements. Then, on July 17, 1987, Lopez made the leap. With $200 in savings, he left his job at the airplane parts factory and turned to comedy full-time. He secured a pair of agents who booked him at small clubs. Without a day job taking up his time, he had more time to put into his act, and he consistently improved.

Within two years, he had new agents and was playing larger clubs, places like the Improv on Melrose in West Hollywood, California. At this famous spot, up-and-coming comedians perform for audiences peppered with agents and other show business professionals looking for fresh talent. One night a particularly prominent audience member saw something special in Lopez's act. Arsenio Hall, who hosted a popular late-night talk show in the late 1980s and early 1990s, was impressed by his performance and offered Lopez the chance to perform on his show.

The marquee of the famous Improv on Melrose comedy club in West Hollywood, California, marks one of the several places Lopez played in the late 1980s and early 1990s on his way to becoming famous.

Hall was not the only person Lopez impressed. A few months later, at a comedy club called the Ice House, Lopez met Ann Serrano, a casting director who became his girlfriend and most avid supporter. She booked talent for events, and asked him to perform at a fund-raising event for the Latino Theatre Lab. Serrano saw in Lopez something even better than talent: a determination to succeed. Backed by people like Hall and Serrano, it seemed that stardom might finally be within Lopez's grasp.

Guest Performer

Lopez made his first appearance on Hall's show in June 1989. He delivered a confident performance and cracked the audience up with the ethnic jokes that would become emblematic of his comedic style. For example, he told the audience that he was a Latino who liked to play golf. "You guys are looking at me like that's ethnically impossible,"[15] he quipped. Lopez became a favorite guest of Hall's, and appeared on the show sixteen times in five years. He thrived on the show's energy. "The place was electric," Lopez said. "It made you want to perform better."[16]

The exposure from Hall's show led to other projects for Lopez, not all of which were well received. For example, he was cast in the 1990 movie *Ski Patrol,* a comedy about a ski crew trying to prevent a developer from ruining their resort. The movie was a flop with both critics and audiences. Rita Kempley of the *Washington Post* panned it for having "lame jokes, dull cast, stale plot."[17] However, it did give Lopez his first movie role and the opportunity to try a comedy medium other than stand-up.

Lopez fared better at the comedy clubs where he continued to deliver stand-up routines. In Chicago, he got laughs by impersonating a Spanish-speaking Rodney Dangerfield and joked about his natural tan. In another performance, he joked about Taco Bell serving salsa in little plastic packets, wiping a fake tear and claiming it was "just like my grandma used to make."[18] He also

The Arsenio Hall Show

Comedian Arsenio Hall hosted a new kind of talk show from 1989–1994. Unlike traditional late-night programs such as *The Tonight Show*, *The Arsenio Hall Show* had an informal format that appealed to younger audiences. The show was particularly popular with African Americans and Latinos. "Arsenio's show was funny, but it was also edgy and confrontational," noted *Newsweek* writer Joshua Alston. "To flip from Johnny Carson [the king of late-night comedy with *The Tonight Show*] to Arsenio was practically intergalactic travel."

The audience cheered, woofed, and delivered fist pumps to inject enthusiasm into the show. Memorable appearances included then presidential candidate Bill Clinton, who played his saxophone on a 1992 episode. Guests came from a wide range of backgrounds, and included country singer Dolly Parton, rapper M.C. Hammer, actor Sylvester Stallone, and basketball star Magic Johnson, who first discussed his HIV-positive status on the show. The show also generated controversy, such as when Hall interviewed Louis Farrakhan, the Nation of Islam leader.

The 100th and final *Arsenio Hall Show* aired on May 27, 1994. Competition from other late-night talk shows hosted by Jay Leno and David Letterman, as well as controversial guests, contributed to its cancellation.

Comedian Arsenio Hall appears on the set of his self-titled talk show, which appealed to young African American and Latino audiences during its 1989–1994 run.

Joshua Alston, "The Crowd in Arsenio's Hall," *Newsweek*, October 29, 2009. www.newsweek.com/2009/10/28/the-crowd-in-arsenio-s-hall.html.

Lopez, top left, appears with others from the cast of Ski Patrol, *his first movie, released in 1990.*

poked fun at the fast-food chain's "Run for the Border" slogan, saying that some Mexicans took it too literally. "Put your luggage down and relax,"[19] he quipped.

He also found favor as a frequent guest on TV shows that featured comedians. He appeared on programs such as *Comic Strip Live*, the *Half Hour Comedy Hour* on MTV, *Sunday Comics*, *VHI Comedy Hour*, and *Evening at the Improv*. He was also a frequent guest on talk shows hosted by celebrities such as Suzanne Somers. He was making $2,000 a week with his standup act and fielding consistent requests for appearances.

However, although he had come a long way from the days when he was juggling comedy with a day job, Lopez was not getting the higher-paying jobs or television show offers he hoped would be the next step in his career. He had achieved some national recognition and was becoming more well known, but the bigger paychecks Lopez had thought would accompany that success were nowhere to be found. He was frustrated, and this led to problems in both his professional and personal life.

Chapter 3

Finding the Right Stuff

By the early 1990s, Lopez faced several professional obstacles. Part of the problem was that Lopez felt he was pigeonholed as a "Latino comic." Booking agents judged him by his name alone and assumed he would pull in a limited audience. "He was everywhere on TV and gaining recognition, but that didn't translate into money in the bank," recalls Ann Lopez, George's girlfriend at the time who later became his wife. "I think George had a lot of anger over the fact that people were labeling him a Latino comedian, and he was just trying to be a comedian."[20]

A Stalled Career

Being billed as a strictly Latino comedian limited the number of roles and comedy projects that Lopez was considered for. There were simply not that many roles that called for Hispanic actors. When Lopez was up for a role or comedy slot that called for a person of Hispanic descent, he was often not the first choice of producers. When Lopez was offered a role, it was often a stereotypical part that he did not want. He turned down parts for gang members, killers, and drug dealers, as well as roles that meanly mocked Hispanics. It was important to Lopez that he not play parts that demeaned his heritage or portrayed Hispanics negatively. "I was offered parts like 'The immigrant with a knife and a body in his trunk' but I wouldn't do it," he says. "I am a comedian first, but I will not wear a sombrero for laughs. There's a line between 'stereotypical' and 'demeaning.'"[21]

Lopez managed to get one conventional movie role, as a detective in the 1993 comedy *Fatal Instinct*. But this small role was the only one he accepted for years. His acting career stalled as he turned down parts he felt betrayed his culture or capitalized on unfair characterizations.

Meanwhile, his stand-up career plateaued. Although he was earning good money—by 1995 he was bringing in more than $100,000 a year—it was not enough. He was surviving as a comedian, but in his own mind was not a success. The venues he played were no bigger or better than those he had performed at in the early 1990s. Lopez was frustrated by his inability to reach the next professional level, and his frustration turned to anger. He envied other comedians who had the widespread exposure and popularity he craved, and obsessed over why he was stuck as a mid-level entertainer. "I think all Latino performers have a chip on their shoulder," he explains. "They don't think their record company's doing enough for them, and they don't think that white people get it, or they think they're being held back because they're Latino. [And] I was one of the angriest."[22]

"Back to Being a Nobody"

Frustrated, angry, and increasingly depressed, Lopez indulged in self-destructive habits. He drank too much and stayed out late when he was on the road. Lopez's anger and self-pity caused his act to grow stale. Each joke felt more unoriginal and impersonal than the last. Audiences did not respond as well to him and he began playing to half-empty rooms. He bombed in Indianapolis, and a critic in California said his show had become ordinary. It became a burden for him to entertain, and he hated criticism. He lost faith in himself and became overwhelmingly negative. "I was back to being a nobody, believing once more that nothing special was ever going to happen to me,"[23] he says.

Lopez was also tiring of the pace of life on the road. He and Ann had married on September 18, 1993, and their daughter, Mayan,

Lopez poses with is wife, Ann, a former casting agent, in 2004. The couple were married in 1993, while Lopez was still struggling to get his career started.

was born in 1995. But Lopez was away from home on gigs every weekend, and he had to take mediocre jobs that involved rigorous travel just to support himself. He was falling into a pattern, becoming a second-rate road comedian, and feared he would never be anything else.

Lopez's anger, frustration, depression, as well as his drinking and partying, eventually affected his relationship with his family. Busy with their newborn daughter, Ann at first did not realize how much he was drinking. When she learned how severely he was abusing alcohol, however, she kicked him out of their house.

A Critical Turning Point

Being thrown out of his home for the second time in his life had a profound impact on Lopez. Personally and professionally, he realized he was at the bottom. He saw that he had made a mess of his family life. He begged his wife to take him back.

She accepted him but told him that she would not tolerate any self-destructive behavior. It was time for Lopez to make drastic changes, and fast.

To help him cope with the anger and negativity that were at the heart of his downward spiral, Lopez began seeing a therapist. In therapy, he learned how his harsh upbringing had shaped his personality. His therapist helped him explore his complicated feelings about his relationship with his grandmother. Lopez realized that the lack of emotional support he received as a child influenced the way he reacted to difficult times as an adult.

The way he was raised had also affected the way he treated his family. It made it difficult for him to believe that he was worthy of their love and kept him from understanding how to show that he loved them. As he puts it, "I didn't know how to love because I didn't see any good examples of it."[24] Lopez cut back on his drinking and partying and made an effort to change his attitude toward his life and family.

A New Life, A New Act

Lopez knew that he had to make changes in his professional life as well if he was going to break out of his rut as a performer. Being angry about the way things were going was getting him nowhere. Therefore, when a manager approached him with some advice after a 1996 appearance at Caroline's Comedy Club in New York City, he listened.

The manager was Dave Becky, who worked with comedian Chris Rock. Becky advised Lopez to reveal more of himself to his audience. While Lopez was good at making clever observations, Becky said making jokes about Mexican fast food could only take his act so far. He needed to adopt a more personal tone. Becky noted that when Rock spoke to an audience, the audience knew his opinion on politics and race; they knew details of Rock's personal life. The result was they felt they knew *him*. Lopez, on the other hand, had difficulty connecting with his audiences precisely because failed to put enough of himself into his act.

Lopez performs on stage in 2005. A decade earlier, he revamped his routine to include more personal jokes based upon his heritage and upbringing, which helped him connect with audiences.

Lopez took Becky's advice. He not only mined his present life for material, but summoned the courage to find humor in his painful childhood memories. He turned his grandmother's cold-hearted treatment into a punch line. In doing so, he created a new and more vibrant act. "I looked at my grandmother, and I looked at my upbringing and I started to talk about that," Lopez says. "Everything completely changed. When I got the information, I went and ran with it really, really hard. It was the one particular thing that really kind of changed me as a comedian."[25]

In his new routines, he created jokes that revolved around his grandmother's denial of Lopez's childhood wants. She constantly said no, he joked, even before she knew what he was asking for. He talked about how they were too poor to have a swimming pool, so his grandmother would watch him spin in a barrel filled with water. He even managed to find humor in his memories of physical discipline from his grandmother. Lopez's humor had a dark edge to it, but his delivery drew laughter.

"A Deeper Type of Comedy"

Lopez also got laughs by incorporating different voices, accents, and characters into his routine. For example, he created a bit that revolved around the way he thought Mexican families reacted when someone did well. In the joke, he enthusiastically offered congratulations in an upper-class Anglo accent, then switched his tone to portray how he said Hispanics really feel. "'So now you think you're all bad or what?'" he joked. "Go to Hallmark and look for that card. We need Mexican greeting cards. The ones in the store are too happy."[26]

Lopez also blended physical humor into his new act. For example, a joke about his relatives' heavy drinking focused on his aunt, who Lopez said ended up at weddings dancing with her dress caught in her pantyhose. To emphasize the punch line, he tucked his suit coat into the back of his pants and imitated the way she shimmied. Lopez's exaggerated movements drew big laughs from audiences.

Finally, Lopez changed the way he joked about cultural differences. Rather than simply making funny observations, such as his old routine that made fun of the "Run for the Border" slogan, he now satirized the way people *reacted* to such situations. In one routine, for example, he depicts a white customer ordering from Hispanic workers at a Jack-in-the-Box restaurant. He used

Lopez delivers his routine in 2004. His decision to include edgy ethnic jokes in his act was viewed by some audiences and critics as controversial.

contrasting accents to emphasize the hilarious lack of communication that might occur in such a situation. "You want one Yumbo Yak with queso with shiz?" the worker asked, baffling the customer. The customer then causes further confusion by asking for a "fountain drink," which the fast-food worker eventually figures out means soda. "Es soda?" he says. "Why not you say soda, stupid?"[27]

No Romance

George Lopez once commented that the best day of his life was the day he met his wife, but he admits he was not very romantic when it came time to propose to Ann. After they had been dating for two years, Ann finally asked if they were going to get married. Lopez simply said, "OK," and Ann went out and bought her own ring.

Ann also took charge of the wedding plans. Lopez said he did little more than agree to be there for the ceremony. Ann set the date and handled the arrangements, and on September 18, 1993, the couple were married at the Mission San Fernando Rey de España in San Fernando, California. Her new husband had a lot to learn about expressing love, she noted. "I have had to teach him that it's okay to be loved and to give love," she said.

Quoted in Susan Horsburgh, "Pool Sharp," *People,* October 21, 2002, p. 129.

Sometimes Lopez's humor pushed the limits of good taste. The thick accent he used in the fast-food routine, for example, made the worker sound uneducated. In another routine, he joked that Mexican families always seem to have one relative in a wheelchair, and how it is always one of the kids' jobs to push the wheelchair.

Most of the time, however, Lopez delicately balanced humor against insults. He claims that all his jokes are done from a place of pride and in the spirit of fun. "Yes, I'm harsh. Yes, I'm putting my own people down," he says. "But … I'm also pushing empowerment. And, really, if we can't laugh at ourselves and others, who's left?"[28] In Lopez's opinion, his controversial brand of ethnic humor is simply the result of growing up in a trying environment. "If you grow up with a supportive family, you become a guy who gets laughs from everyday observations: laundry and airplanes and relationships," he says. "If you grow up emotionally neglected, you do a deeper type of comedy."[29]

Recordings, Radio, and Roles

Lopez's new material resonated with both audiences and critics. It became easier for audiences to relate to him as a real person, rather than an impersonal entertainer. "What's appealing about his tales is how candid they are," wrote Marissa Rodriguez in *Hispanic* magazine. "Through all the drama and deprivation, the stories are hilarious, poignant and personal. And, he does this without ever sacrificing authenticity."[30] Lopez seemed to have broken out of the rut he had been stuck in for so long. His confidence grew and he began playing bigger and better venues, often as the top act of the night. His routines were even turned into comedy albums—he released *Alien Nation* in 2000 and *Right Now, Right Now* in 2001.

In 2000, after a guest appearance on the Rick Dees radio show, he accepted a full-time gig as an LA radio show host. In doing so he became the first Latino to host a major English-language morning show in Los Angeles. This position both exposed him to

Lopez, far right, poses with the director and cast of his 2000 movie Bread and Roses, *including from left Ken Loach, Elpidia Carrillo, Adrien Brody, and Pilar Padilla.*

a larger audience and offered him a break from life on the road. He took over the 5 A.M. to 9 A.M. slot and entertained morning commuters with his unique style of comedy. Because his ratings were not as high as the station managers wanted them to be, the job lasted less than a year. By then, however, Lopez had plenty of other projects to turn to.

Lopez returned to movies in 2000 with a role in *Bread and Roses,* a part that his wife encouraged him to audition for. The movie examined the working conditions of primarily Hispanic workers who clean office buildings. Lopez played the part of Perez, a manager, who is caught in the middle of a janitor's strike. Thanks to the many jobs he had held in his life, Lopez knew exactly how to portray the character. He drew on the way he had been treated by past bosses to bring a specific kind of anger and meanness to the role. The point of the film was to show that janitorial workers were woefully underpaid, and the plot focused on the plight of an illegal immigrant. For Lopez, the movie was important because it gave him the opportunity to act for the first time in a decade.

Some critics thought the film was too heavy-handed, and it did not do well at the box office. However, critic Roger Ebert of the *Chicago Sun-Times* said the film delivered an important message about service workers who often do not get enough credit for what they do. In his review, he encouraged moviegoers to think about the role these people played in their everyday lives: "Will this move change anything, or this review make you want to see it? No, probably not. But when you come in tomorrow morning, someone will have emptied your wastebasket."[31]

Lopez also had a role in the 2002 movie *Real Women Have Curves.* The film starred America Ferrera as a Mexican American high school senior from East Los Angeles who confronts weight and body-image issues as she seeks independence from her close-knit family. Lopez plays a teacher who encourages Ferrera's character to attend college. Although the film was not one of the top-grossing movies of the year, it received positive reviews. For example, critic Lisa Schwarzbaum of *Entertainment Weekly* called the movie a "vibrant, welcoming family drama."[32]

The Break of a Lifetime

Lopez's career enjoyed another boost one night as he performed at the Improv in Brea, California. For the second time in his career, his act impressed an influential audience member: actress Sandra Bullock. Bullock was at the Improv with a specific goal: to find the star of a Hispanic television show she hoped to produce. Most television shows featured white actors, and Bullock—who owns a production company called Fortis Films—wanted to create a show that focused on a family from a different cultural group. When she saw Lopez perform, she knew she had found an actor who could help her create that type of show.

Actress Turned Producer

Actress Sandra Bullock, who was the first to insist that George Lopez star in his own television show, initially found stardom as a film star. She won acclaim for the 1994 film *Speed* and formed her own production company, Fortis Films, in the late 1990s. Through Fortis she produced *Hope Floats* (1998), *Miss Congeniality* (2000), and *Miss Congeniality 2: Armed and Fabulous* (2005), in all of which she also had a starring role. She has also appeared in many movies that she has not produced, and in 2010 won the Academy Award for Best Actress for her role in *The Blind Side*.

Lopez and Sandra Bullock, right, appear at the People's Choice Awards in 2010.

Bullock was impressed by Lopez's material as well as his appearance and character—his authenticity and his unrestrained delivery made him just what she was looking for. "You can see he fought to get where he is, yet he is hilarious," says Bullock. "He has a way of hiding his pain, but you can also see it."[33] Bullock believed Lopez's act had the potential to carry a television series. His comedy was tinged with enough pain to make it meaningful, yet his jokes still provoked side-splitting laughter. Bullock thought the dramatic moments that formed the basis of Lopez's jokes had the potential to become sitcom storylines.

The opportunity to secure a TV deal was the big break he had been dreaming about. It took about a decade longer than he had hoped it would, but Lopez was finally going to get a shot at stardom.

Chapter 4

George Lopez Breaks New Ground

The show Bullock produced would give Lopez more than the opportunity to be a star. It would also give him the chance to positively portray Mexican Americans. He had previously rejected roles that were based on negative Hispanic stereotypes, but here was an opportunity to base a television show around a wholesome Hispanic family, one that had much in common with any other working-class American family as well as unique cultural differences. In addition, he wanted to highlight the important—and growing—role Latinos played in American society. Too often, he thought, they were portrayed by network executives, producers, directors, and writers as an inferior underclass. "They see us as the help," he said. "They see us as the people who raise their kids, cut their grass and cook their food, but not as their friends or equals."[34]

Lopez hoped to create a television show that told the story of a family that was not perfect but whose members ultimately cared about each other. This is a typical sitcom premise, but it had never been successfully done with a Hispanic family. If Lopez could do it, he would truly be breaking new ground.

A Hard Sell

There was much work to be done before the show could begin taping episodes, however. Lopez worked with producers and writers to develop plot lines based on both his childhood and

Sandra Bullock, left, and Lopez take questions at the Television Critics Association Press Tour in 2002 to promote George Lopez.

adult life. Lopez would play a manager in an airplane parts factory, similar to a position he had held as a struggling comic early in his career. He would have a Cuban American wife, just as he did in real life. His character had two children (although in real life Lopez had one) and a best friend named Ernie. Adding much of the humor to the sitcom would be his character's mother, who was based on Lopez's real-life grandmother.

Bullock loved the show's concept and its script. She enthusiastically met with network executives to try and make a deal. However, she was surprised by how difficult the show was to sell. She had considerable clout in Hollywood, thanks to such successful films as *Miss Congeniality* and *Speed*. She even offered to appear in several episodes of *George Lopez* as Accident Amy, a stumbling coworker of George's. Despite this, finding a network that was willing put to the show on the air was much harder than she expected.

Lopez, however, was less surprised. He anticipated it would not be easy to convince a network that a show about a Hispanic family was worth putting on their weekly schedule. Getting a show on the air often comes down to knowing the right people, and Latinos, said Lopez, were often not close enough to the people who made those decisions to get their programs on broadcast television. He had worked in stand-up comedy for years before Bullock noticed him and gave him the chance to develop a show. "It's an exclusive club," he said. "Directors and writers and producers rehire each other when a show fails. And the majority of them are Anglo. To get in and be of color takes a long time."[35]

After much perseverance, an executive at ABC offered Bullock and Lopez a chance to prove that their show could work. He offered to put the show on the air for four weeks in March and April 2002. The limited run of *George Lopez* would replace another show that had not been doing well in the ratings. If it went over well with audiences, more episodes could be ordered.

Bullock and Lopez had mixed feelings about ABC's offer. They were excited about making it to the TV lineup. But they had been aiming for the show to be picked up for the fall 2002 season. The spring air date meant they had to scramble to find writers, a cast, and directors. Furthermore, being approved for just four shows meant that the team had a limited time to prove they could deliver a successful series. The show's failure would not only have an immediate impact on the cast and crew, but could also hurt the chances for future shows with Hispanic casts to make it on the air. "If we failed, we would have been the people that kept everyone else from jumping in the water,"[36] said Bruce Helford, an executive producer of *George Lopez*. There was pressure, but also a rich reward at stake.

Good Enough for Laughs

Lopez admits that the first shows were not perfect. A different director and different writers were used for each episode. The cast was just getting used to working together. Furthermore, Lopez

Lopez appears at the ABC Primetime Preview Weekend in 2002 to tout George Lopez as a part of the network's fall program schedule.

was not a trained actor; he had a comic's, not an actor's, technique. He relied too much, for example, on widening his eyes to convey expressions or to punctuate a joke. However, his comic timing was good enough to deliver punch lines. Bullock's guest appearance also added a spark to the show, as she slipped on a chair while changing a light bulb and twisted her hair in a fan when she confused it with a phone.

The show only had a brief time to prove itself, but it made an impact in the ratings. Its first episode pulled in 10.4 million viewers and won its time slot in the all-important 18-to-49-year-old viewing bracket. "ABC ... may have a new hit in 'The George Lopez Show,'"[37] noted *People* writer Stephen M. Silverman. The show attracted an average of 9 million viewers per episode during its short spring run, but Lopez had to wait months to learn the fate of his show. In August he finally got the call: the network wanted 13 more episodes of *George Lopez*.

Laughter with Substance

The show had a working-class setting and was meant to portray Lopez's life as it might have been if he had chosen some other career. It also focused on the foibles of the typical American dad, such as George's getting into trouble when he invades his daughter's privacy by reading her online chats. Family concerns, such as his daughter's troubles with boys and her friends, and his wife's adoption of a sickly dog, also figured into the program's plots.

The show wove many of Lopez's real-life experiences into the plot, such as his lack of childhood birthday parties and his mundane factory jobs. Other details from Lopez's own life served as jumping-off points for the show's plots. During one episode, for example, his character begins a search for his absent father. The lack of affection Lopez had received as a child was also a central theme of the show.

The crucial difference, however, between Lopez's real life and harsh upbringing and *George Lopez* is that on TV, situations were

Belita Moreno, left, plays Lopez's character's mother and Constance Marie his wife on the set of George Lopez. *Aspects of Moreno's character, Benny, were based on Lopez's real-life grandmother.*

Not Happiness, but Forgiveness

Lopez consistently recalls his childhood as difficult and loveless, but his grandmother remembered it differently. In a 2002 interview with *New York Times* reporter Mireya Navarro, Benita Gutierrez said she considered his upbringing to be normal. Although Lopez said she never expressed approval of him, Gutierrez told Navarro, "I'm proud of him, very proud."[1]

Gutierrez did not find fault with the way she was portrayed on Lopez's television show. She knew that the character of George's mother, a woman with a mean streak and a sharp tongue, was based on her. She even conceded that it was an accurate depiction. However, she laughed when she watched the show and thought the character was funny.

Though Lopez and his grandmother saw life differently, Lopez continued to care about her until her death in 2009. She was not a warm, loving person, but Lopez eventually learned to forgive her for the way she treated him. "I have come to understand that I cannot expect someone who doesn't feel to feel," he says. "She never knew joy or how to express it."[2]

1. Quoted in Mireya Navarro," A Life So Sad He Had to Be Funny," *New York Times,* November 27, 2002. www.nytimes.com/2002/11/27/arts/life-so-sad-he-had-be-funny-george-lopez-mines-rich-vein-gloom-with-all-latino.html.

2. Quoted in James Poniewozik and Jeanne McDowell, "Prime-Time Therapy," *Time,* March 24, 2003, p. 64.

mostly played for laughs. For example, during one episode in which George is told he must fire his mother from her factory job, he says, "You want me to fire my mom? I get scared wishing her a happy birthday."[38] His mother's personality as a tough-love parent was also exaggerated for laughs. For example, in one scene, everyone looks frightened when she walks into a room with a sharp knife—until she asks who wants some cake. In another, George tries to comfort his daughter by noting how he was also made fun of as a child. In a warm voice, he remembers how as a child he was told, "'You're stupid, you're fat, your father's a loser.'" He then realizes suddenly, "Your grandmother can be very cruel!"[39]

It was important to Lopez that he portray Hispanics as capable, valuable people who could succeed on their own merits. For example, in one episode, George is recruited for another job at a different company, but becomes concerned at his interview when he is shown only the executive dining room, gym, and putting green, not the actual factory where he will work if hired. He realizes that the company only wants to hire him to fill their minority quota. Offended that the company does not care whether he can do the job, he returns to his old company. L. Brent Bozell III, a writer for *Insight on the News*, applauded the way the show depicted the problem and the way George resolved it: "It's a message about universal human aspirations toward an American Dream."[40]

A Milestone for TV

In addition to picking up an additional 13 episodes in 2003, ABC renewed the show for the 2003–2004 season. *George Lopez* averaged 10.4 million viewers during its first full season on the air, and when Bullock again guest-starred in November it drew more than 11 million viewers. Of those viewers, an estimated 1.1 million were Hispanic. Although *George Lopez* was not one of the highest-rated programs of the season, it fared better than two other sitcoms featuring Hispanics that aired in 2002: *Luis*, starring Luis Guzman, and *The Ortegas*, with Cheech Marin. The latter received disappointing reviews from critics and was pulled from the air after a few weeks. *Luis*, meanwhile, featured an overly aggressive performance by Guzman and tried too hard to wring laughs from crude humor and superficial ethnic jokes.

Lopez, on the other hand, consciously avoided that type of stereotypical humor in favor of a more mainstream approach, and it worked. *George Lopez* pulled in a broad, multicultural audience, and as a result became the first successful network sitcom

The cast of George Lopez included from left Valente Rodriguez, Luis Armand Garcia, Constance Marie, Emiliano Diez, Belita Moreno, Lopez, and Masiela Lusha.

to feature an all-Latino cast. "This was a pretty big deal, that they would put this on the air and the show would stick with [mainstream] audiences," Helford said. "To make this kind of breakthrough is enormous."[41]

Indeed, *George Lopez* was applauded for rejecting stereotypes that portrayed Hispanics as either negative or insignificant characters. "*George Lopez* is ... a refreshing contrast to the usual portrayal of Latinos in film and television as recent immigrants, victims or criminals,"[42] wrote Mireya Navarro in the *New York Times*. John

Markert of Columbia University agreed, observing that the show was "decidedly not the same old Hispano." Markert liked that at the show's core was a loving family grappling with real-world issues: "Such a portrait is likely to promote pride among fellow Latinos at the same time that it challenges some of the stereotypes about poor, rural, illegal immigrant Hispanics that are so pervasive within the wider society."[43]

George Lopez also placed Latinos in mainstream culture by aligning them with ordinary Americans who face common family and professional issues. Indeed, even though it featured a Mexican American family and spotlit Latino culture, the show was primarily about a working-class American family dealing with daily life and all its trials. For example, George's tense but funny relationship with his mother was one of the plotlines that Americans from all walks of life could relate to. Fights between children and parents was another, as George's character argued with his daughter over her choice of boyfriends. "The humor is character driven, not culturally driven," explains Ann Lopez. "It definitely has Latino references, celebrations, flavor, and slang, but the stories could be about any family in America."[44]

Acting Improves but Ratings Disappoint

By the third season of the show, Lopez had improved measurably as a performer. "Initially, he seemed uncomfortable in front of the camera; with his hyper-exuberance and exaggerated delivery, Lopez the actor made Lopez the show feel like an overrehearsed stand-up routine," said reviewer Ross Dalton of *Entertainment Weekly*. "But now Lopez seems more at ease in his studio setting and far more believable as a television dad."[45]

At the start of the show's third season, Lopez felt satisfied with his life and career. Gone were his frustration, anger, and depression. "I've gotten to a place where I am comfortable and I don't battle myself," he said at the time. "I'm further ahead than I ever thought I'd be. I've exceeded everyone's expectations—including, I think, my own."[46]

Lopez poses on the set of George Lopez, the success of which gave him a sense of satisfaction with his life and career.

Real-Life Search

Lopez's search for his father was not merely a plot line for his television show. He sought out his father in real life, too. Lopez and his wife first tried to track him down themselves, and then hired a private investigator.

After these efforts failed to locate his father, Lopez realized he did not care to look any more. "I've stopped looking for my dad," he says. "He was never alive, never lived in my life, not for a second, so why would I start a relationship now? Some things are better left undone."

George Lopez with Armen Keteyian, *Why You Crying?* New York: Touchstone, 2004, p. 185.

Lopez's show continued to explore issues relating to work and family life, always in a humorous way. George's teenage daughter dealt with boyfriend issues, his wife started her own business, and his son struggled in school. George's relationship with his mother remained a central theme, and heavier plot lines explored issues such as alcoholism, impoverished Cuban and Haitian immigrants, and health problems.

In season three, however, the show's ratings started to slip. The program was moved to different nights and timeslots to renew its appeal, but that seemed to make it hard for casual viewers to find. The show had jumped from 70th to 58th place in its first two seasons, but fell to 96th place in its third season. Although it rebounded to 79th the next year, it failed to climb higher. Its audience eventually shrank to 6.1 million per episode.

The slip was also due to changing viewer tastes. *George Lopez* was not the only sitcom to suffer in the ratings. Networks and viewers began to prefer reality television to situation comedies. Programs such as *American Idol, Survivor, Extreme Home Makeover*, and *Dancing with the Stars* dominated the ratings, edging out more expensive and more traditional programming. Networks put energy and money into these new shows rather than family comedies. In addition, some viewers just no longer found the show funny. When the program came back on the air in January 2007 after a break of a few weeks, reviewer Robert Bianco lamented, "ABC sitcom fortunes go from bad to worse with the return of *George Lopez*."[47]

After five seasons, *George Lopez* was cancelled. Lopez was disappointed that he would not be able to wrap up the show's storylines with a final season. More importantly, he regarded the cancellation of *George Lopez* as a blow to the diversity of network television. "TV just became really, really, white again,"[48] he said. He was particularly offended that the network chose to pick up a show called *Cavemen* after it cancelled *Lopez*. "So a Chicano can't be on TV," he said, "but a caveman can?"[49]

A Second Life in Syndication

As it turns out, Lopez got a second chance to prove his show was a hit. *George Lopez* began appearing in syndication on the cable channel Nickelodeon in 2008 and improved that network's overall ratings. In 2008, *George Lopez* helped bring the network's evening programming, called Nick at Nite, to the top of the ratings among adults aged eighteen to forty-nine. This was an improvement of 50 percent over the previous year. The show became a popular sitcom on local broadcast stations as well. Local stations could purchase reruns of the show to air, and those that did were pleasantly surprised at how many people tuned in. Because so many people discovered the show after it had been cancelled, *Broadcasting and Cable* magazine described *George Lopez* as "a sleeper hit."[50]

Nickelodeon executives were happy to have Lopez's show on their schedule, as it fit perfectly in its family-viewing niche. "*George Lopez* is the epitome of the modern family in many ways," said Cyma Zarghami, president of Nickelodeon/MTVN Kids and Family Group. "It's a modern couple working hard, two modern kids who talk to them the way modern kids talk to parents, and it was a great show that got seen by very few people when it was on the [ABC] network."[51] The network actually thought of *Lopez's*

George Lopez, with its cast of, from left, Belita Moreno, Constance Marie, Masiela Lusha, Lopez, and Luis Armand Garcia, was a popular addition to Nickelodeon's Nick at Nite programming when it went into syndication in 2008.

modest broadcast ratings as an asset, because more of its viewers regarded the show as new programming.

Lopez had achieved his goal of creating a popular family show that attracted a multicultural audience. He helped bring Latino culture into the mainstream, and reinforced the idea that Hispanics were ordinary Americans who faced the same issues people of any culture did. Lopez broke away from the way Hispanics had traditionally been portrayed and helped Americans see Hispanics in a more positive light.

Chapter 5

Making an Impact

As Lopez's celebrity grew, he was asked to appear on awards shows, in movies, and even on a football pregame show. Far from the second-rate comedian he feared he would become, Lopez was now a star. Lopez did not simply bask in the limelight, however. He used his celebrity to advance the same messages he delivered in his television program. In all of his actions, he emphasized Latino pride, and for this received both applause and criticism.

Walking a Fine Line

In his comedy, Lopez walks a fine line. His jokes risk offending people of both Mexican American and other ethnic and cultural heritage. To keep his Latino fans and remain authentic, he tends to present jokes from a Hispanic point of view. Yet he also wants to appeal to, not alienate, people from mainstream and other minority groups. To this end, Lopez gears some of his material specifically toward his Spanish-speaking audience, but makes the majority of his jokes something people of any culture can find humorous.

For example, in the 2002 movie *The Original Latin Kings of Comedy*, which presented the live-performance stand-up comedy acts of a number of Chicano comedians, Lopez made fun of two cultures to get a laugh. He began his routine by speaking in a mixture of Spanish and English. Knowing that some members of the audience did not speak Spanish, he made a joke about how the only people confused were the English speakers. He then kept

Lopez appears in a mariachi costume while hosting the Latin Grammy Awards in 2004. His jokes routinely poke fun at stereotypes and other aspects of Hispanic culture.

the rest of his act in English, and went into a routine about how Mexican Americans say hello by nodding their head. His rapid nods and body language drew laughs from the audience.

In other routines, Lopez has skewered white Americans for pigeonholing Latinos into certain types of jobs. One of his favorite jokes revolves around the notion that white people stereotype Latinos as groundskeepers, and someday this will come back to haunt them. "In 2015 they say that the largest majority of people will be Latino and you'll tell scary stories to your grandkids," he jokes. "'A long time ago when I was growing up, there used to be people who were white,' and the kid says, 'Really?' and you say, 'Yeah, like the man who cuts our grass.'"[52]

Lopez also pokes fun at his own culture, and frequently turns cultural quirks into punch lines. In one episode of *George Lopez*, for example, George's wife says his head would make a good piñata. In another, George asks why his children need to learn to swim when they are already in the United States, a reference to Mexicans who swim across canals and rivers to illegally enter the country. He also joked that he once got so hungry he ate the beans in a bean bag chair. In his stand-up act, he plays to the stereotype that Mexicans are poor, and jokes that his family created wading pools by flooding an uneven cement patio.

Lopez delivers edgy ethnic jokes, but not, he says, out of anger or resentment. He views his act as a series of observations about life, and about how Hispanic culture fits into mainstream America. "I connect with people, I think, because it's so real and it's not false," he says. "And I don't think that they're really jokes as much as recollections."[53]

Not Everyone Is Laughing

Lopez's brand of comedy is not without its critics. By engaging in ethnic humor, he risks reinforcing the very stereotypes he resents, such as that Mexicans enter the country illegally or eat only rice and beans. Ann Lopez is among the people who think sometimes his humor goes too far. She also thinks his stand-up act is sometimes too hard on Hispanics. For example, she was unhappy

Lopez performs on stage in 2007. His act has been criticized by those who think his ethnic humor is sometimes too crude or mean-spirited.

with his appearance at the 2003 Emmy Awards show, where he joked about the extremely good-looking women delivering the news on Spanish-language television shows. He also made fun of Hispanic families who let relatives live in their garage, and made crude jokes about eating deep-fried tripe (the lining of a cow's stomach) with chili, a traditional Mexican dish called menudo. "In my opinion," she said, "those jokes were not the intelligent humor that George Lopez is known for."[54]

Some critics also find fault with Lopez's stand-up act, and are turned off by his Latino-centered comedy and his emphasis on the power of Latino people. Writer Pete Allman, for example, admires Lopez for being talented, energetic, and funny, but thinks some of his observations are off-base. He notes that while Lopez can sell out shows, the content of his act does not always resonate with people who are not Latino. "Slamming white people and promising that Latinos have all but taken over the United States gets some huge laughs, like having the white guy mow the lawn. Seems so crazy that it's funny, I guess," he says sarcastically. "Just as funny as beating your kid when he wants to have a birthday party or how stupid whites are for talking about their kids going to college or trying to keep their kids from being hurt."[55]

Lopez's satirical look at the differences between Hispanic and Anglo culture and his observations about cultural stereotypes do not always go over well with audiences, either. For example, at one performance, some people booed when he noted in his monologue that more babies will be born to minorities than to whites in the United States. Jokes about how white people would have to learn to clean their own house got a similarly chilly reception.

Lopez realizes that some of his comments sting, but insists he only says what is true. As he puts it, "I love comedy and I love people, but you have to say things that are the truth, and sometimes the truth hurts."[56] He claims his goal is not to put down any particular race or ethnicity, but rather fight against ignorance and stereotyping. He thinks the best way to do this is to encourage people to laugh at themselves rather than make fun of others. While comedians have to be sensitive to their audience's viewpoint, Lopez believes comedy about ethnic and racial differences is possible if it is done in the right spirit: "If you do it out of meanness, it's no fun."[57]

Canadian television critic John Doyle thinks Lopez has struck the right balance. He has noted that Lopez does not hurt anyone with his humor and makes observations that all people can appreciate. "It's all very gentle, really," Doyle said. "Even when Lopez delves into politics he's not cutting and he's not hurting anybody.... He manages to be respectful without sentimentalizing his subjects."[58]

In Demand

Although, and perhaps because, Lopez is controversial, he remains a sought-after performer. His quick wit and delivery have made him a popular choice for hosting and presenting at awards shows. Lopez made a number of such appearances in 2003, when he was a presenter at the American Music Awards, hosted the Latin Grammy Awards, and was one of eleven comedians to host the Emmy Awards. Also in 2003 he was a presenter at the People's Choice Awards, hosted a benefit for the Latino Theater Company in Los Angeles, cohosted the Walt Disney World Christmas Day parade, appeared on the *Hollywood Squares* daytime television game show numerous times, and was hired by the HBO cable network to provide humor on its *Inside the NFL* football show. Lopez's stand-up act took him on the road as well, including a performance at an event at the Ford Theater in Washington, D.C., with President George W. Bush and First Lady Laura Bush in the audience.

Over the years Lopez has also appeared on the Nickelodeon Kids' Choice Awards and the Fox network's Teen Choice Awards. His 2010 appearance on the Teen Choice Awards was one of the show's highlights. He lampooned the Kardashian family reality television series by dressing as a new sister, "Cougar Kardashian." He also poked fun at teen idol Justin Bieber when he gave out an award, saying that his high heels were so tight that he had a blister the size of Bieber.

Lopez has continued to do stand-up even as his career has expanded, and has released several live-performance CDs.

Lopez appears dressed as "Cougar Kardashian" at the 2010 Teen Choice Awards, accompanied by, from left, Kourtney Kardashian, Khloe Kardashian, and Kim Kardashian.

In 2006, *El Mas Chingnon* (*The Baddest*) was released, followed by *America's Mexican* (2007). He sold out the AT&T Center in San Antonio, Texas, for his television special *Tall, Dark, and Chicano,* which was broadcast on HBO in August 2009 and released as a DVD. Lopez has continued to maintain a presence on television and in movies, too. He appeared on nine episodes of the television show *Dancing with the Stars* in 2006 and 2007, in the 2006 movie *Where's Marty,* and in the 2007 films *Balls of Fury* and *Tortilla Heaven.*

Member of an Elite Club

Lopez's success has made him rich, and nowhere is his change in status more evident than on the golf course. As a kid he lobbed fruit out of his backyard with a couple of old clubs, but by 2007 he was a member of the upper-crust Lakeside Golf Club in Burbank, California, playing golf alongside celebrities such as Kevin Costner, Jack Nicholson, and Sylvester Stallone. In 1999

Lopez golfs at Pebble Beach in 2010. His success has allowed him to play at some of the game's most exclusive courses and charity tournaments.

he had visited California's exclusive and expensive Pebble Beach golf courses to buy souvenirs, but in 2003 he bought a home alongside one of the courses. These courses host major golf tournaments such as the U.S. Open and the AT&T Pebble Beach National Pro-Am, which features celebrity players such as quarterback Tom Brady, musician Vince Gill, and actor Andy Garcia, as well as professional golfers.

In 2004, Lopez became part of that elite group. Actor Clint Eastwood invited him to play in the AT&T tournament, and he was paired with professional golfer Jesper Parnevik. The duo finished third, and Lopez brought more than his golf skill to the tournament. He added comic relief during the tournament as well. He joked that when he and his partner were golfing with fellow Latino Andy Garcia, they thought about putting another Latino in their group, "but three Latinos is a gang."[59] He also poked fun at stereotypes of Mexicans as lawn caretakers when a person began loudly mowing the lawn at a home beside the fairway and disrupted his concentration. "You'd think the Mexicans would try to help me!"[60] he quipped.

Lopez also brought his sense of humor to the Bob Hope Chrysler Classic in 2007, when he became the first celebrity to host the event since Hope died in 2003. He took the opportunity to make jokes that are emblematic of his style, saying, "Let's be honest, the sight of a Latino with a club in his hand scares people."[61] To Lopez, though, these were just jokes; he says he has always been treated with respect on the course. As he told a *Golf Digest* writer, "I know the golf community is conservative, but it just seems that on a golf course, people like each other."[62]

Golf was one of the ways in which Lopez realized he has become a model for others. He once had the opportunity to play a round at Pebble Beach with professional golfer Lee Trevino, a fellow Mexican American and Lopez's boyhood idol. A crowd of maintenance workers gathered to watch them play. "I realized that, in a way, Lee and I were walking symbols of opportunity for these men, who were working so hard to prepare the course—and to create a better life for their families,"[63] Lopez commented. When someone asked if Lopez and Trevino would have their photo taken with the workers, they posed around a lawnmower with the group. The driver's seat was

Growing Through Golf

Golf has been not just a favorite pastime for Lopez, but also a form of therapy. From golf he has learned the importance of not getting upset, remaining calm, and staying focused. During his early years in the game, he would get very upset if he played poorly. He would throw, break, and bury clubs. He would quit and walk off the course if he was doing poorly. As he came to terms with his life and career, however, he also matured on the golf course and was able to focus on the game. The discipline the game required helped him grow as a person. "Golf is the father I never had," he said. "When I look at my 14 clubs, I think of each one of them as a teacher and role model."

Quoted in Jamie Diaz, "G-Lo," *Golf Digest,* February 2008, p. 104.

Lopez pauses on the scenic greens of Pebble Beach in 2009. He credits the game of golf with teaching him patience, focus, and discipline.

left empty to symbolize that everyone was equal and that anyone could become a success no matter where they started out. Lopez and Trevino each has a framed copy of the photo in his home.

Model Comedian

Indeed, Lopez has become a role model in several ways. His is a true rags-to-riches story that has inspired others to achieve their dreams. Lopez has made a conscious decision to be a performer whom younger Hispanics can look up to. As a child, Lopez had admired Freddie Prinze, but Prinze's time in the spotlight had been fleeting, and since Prinze's time few Hispanic actors had become major stars. It was important to Lopez to give Hispanics a valuable role model. As he puts it, "It's nice for a kid who's eight years old to see somebody like me and think, 'If he can do it, I can do it.'"[64] Ann Lopez thinks her husband's accomplishments instill a sense of pride in young Latinos. "It shows them that they count," she says. "The impact of these positive images will hopefully give our Latino children the inspiration to dream big dreams and achieve their goals."[65]

Lopez has worked to promote Latino pride in a variety of ways. For example, in 2008 he narrated an educational video about the late Mexican American labor activist Cesar Chavez. He also participated in the documentary *Brown Is the New Green: George Lopez and the American Dream*, which was broadcast on PBS in 2007. The documentary stressed the importance of Latinos in America and took a behind-the-scenes look at Lopez's life and career. Latino pride is also an ongoing feature of his stand-up act. He was proud when fourteen thousand people came to see him in 2009 at the AT&T Center, even in the middle of a recession. In his act he applauded Sonia Sotomayor, the nation's first Hispanic Supreme Court justice.

Charitable Celebrity

Lopez supports his community in more tangible ways as well. In 2009, Lopez and his wife started their own foundation, the Ann and George Lopez Foundation. Through this organization, they help underprivileged children and adults. Lopez knows what it is like to grow up in a poor community and uses his foundation to support education and health care in low-income areas. The organization has sponsored summer camps and family camp weekends in Lake Hughes, California, for children impacted by kidney disease and has also sponsored a holiday party and toy drive at San Fernando Elementary School. Lopez raises money for his foundation with an annual golf outing, which attracts

Lopez performs at Help Haiti with George Lopez and Friends, an event he organized in 2010 to raise funds for victims of the earthquake in Haiti.

stars such as Dennis Quaid, Tim Allen, Cedric the Entertainer, and Hillary Duff.

Lopez takes a worldwide approach to his charity. In 2010, he threw a benefit concert called "Help Haiti with George Lopez and Friends." The event, at the Nokia Center in Los Angeles, featured celebrities such as Andy Garcia, Margaret Cho, and Samuel L. Jackson and raised money for victims of the 2009 Haitian earthquake. It was not the first time Lopez reached out

A Fan of *Dancing with the Stars*

The reality television show *Dancing with the Stars* pulls in millions of viewers, and George Lopez is one of them. He avidly watches the show that pairs celebrities with professional dancers. Each week the pairs compete before judges and TV audiences for the best dance of the evening, and each week, a losing pair is voted off the show until only the winning couple is left.

Lopez appeared on nine episodes of *Dancing with the Stars* in 2006 and 2007 and also enjoyed watching the show with his family. In spring 2010, his family was so amused by reality TV star Kate Gosselin's cringe-worthy dancing that he encouraged viewers to vote to keep her on the air. As a guest on the *Larry King Live* talk show, Lopez called her performance "a train wreck you cannot turn away from" and urged viewers to vote to keep her on the show so he could keep enjoying it with his family. "I watched with my wife, my daughter, the dogs in the bed," he said. "It was like a Norman Rockwell painting. Only Kate Gosselin has been able to make that happen in my house. I'm not ready for that to end."

His campaign did not work, however. Gosselin was voted off of the show, and singer Nicole Scherzinger of the Pussycat Dolls took home the prize at the end of the season.

Quoted in *Larry King Live*, "Bill Cosby Takes On Bullying; Lopez Discusses Conan Moving to TBS," April 13, 2010. http://archives.cnn.com/TRANSCRIPTS/1004/13/lkl.01.html.

to others around the world. He also assisted victims of the 2001 El Salvador and Guatemala earthquake and in 2004 was named the Honorary Mayor of Los Angeles for his efforts, as Los Angeles is home to a large number of immigrants from El Salvador.

Lopez's charitable efforts in the San Fernando Valley also earned him the Manny Mota Foundation Community Spirit Award in 2001. He was the recipient of the People for the American Way award in 2004. Also in 2004, he received a Humanitarian Award from the Harvard Foundation for his work with organizations such as the Stop the Violence program and for work with the Los Angeles Police Department. Allen Counter, director of the foundation, said of Lopez, "He is one of the most widely admired artists in America and a model source of inspiration for young people of all backgrounds."[66]

In 2005, *Time* magazine named Lopez one of the "25 Most Influential Hispanics in America." He was honored for being one of the only three Latinos, along with Desi Arnaz of *I Love Lucy* fame and Prinze, to lead a network sitcom, as well as for overcoming a difficult childhood to achieve success. Lopez does not take such honors lightly, and uses his success to encourage other Latinos not just to dream, but to plan. Latinos, he says, should have "goals, not just dreams. What is a dream to Mexican kids, to white kids is a goal."[67] It is important to Lopez that young Hispanic Americans know they can achieve success in whatever endeavors they put their minds to.

Chapter 6

No Backing Down

Lopez has proven that a Latino can achieve success in the entertainment world, but his success has not necessarily meant that his life is easy. He has faced life-or-death health issues and has been presented with new career challenges. Lopez has risen to these challenges and started new ventures by employing the hard-working, tough attitude that has helped him overcome barriers in the past.

Medical Emergency

By 2004, Lopez had a solid, successful career. Both his television show and stand-up comedy career were popular and lucrative, and he was putting energy into charitable ventures and guest appearances as well. However, he was hiding the fact that health problems were making life difficult and painful for him every day.

Lopez's health began to fail in his forties, when a condition that had been with him since childhood turned critical. Since he was seventeen, Lopez had suffered from high blood pressure, which can be a symptom of kidney problems. The job of the kidneys is to filter the body's blood and excrete waste in the form of urine. After waste and extra fluid are taken out of the blood, the urine flows to the bladder through tubes called ureters.

Kidney Transplants

In 2005, Lopez underwent a kidney transplant that saved his life. Kidney transplant surgery usually lasts three to five hours, with the patient under general anesthesia. Patients spend three to five days in the hospital after the operation. There is pain and soreness around the area where an incision was made, but the new kidney often starts to work right away. In some cases, it may take a few weeks to begin functioning. About 95 percent of the time, the new kidney is still working well after a year, according to the National Kidney Foundation. People who have received a kidney transplant need to take medication for the rest of their life to keep their immune system from attacking the new organ.

About sixteen thousand people receive a kidney transplant each year, but not everyone who needs an organ transplant is fortunate enough to receive one. According to the National Kidney Foundation, eighteen people die each day waiting for the transplant of a vital organ. This could be a kidney, heart, lung, pancreas, liver, or bone marrow.

In Lopez's body, an abnormality he had been born with caused his ureters to narrow. As a result, waste was not easily excreted from his body. Instead it flowed backward and was poisoning his kidneys.

Lopez also suffered from chronic fatigue. Although fatigue is a symptom of worsening kidney disease, Lopez did not take it as a warning sign because he did not know he was sick. He rarely went to the doctor, despite his health problems. "Latinos, we only go to the doctor when we are bleeding," he has said. "We forget about things internal. Fatigue is just fatigue."[68]

A cultural reluctance to visit the doctor had been something he had joked about in his standup routine, but his situation was anything but funny. After he began experiencing unbearable pain, he could not deny he needed medical care. A visit to the doctor revealed that Lopez's kidney problems were so severe that his survival depended on a kidney transplant. His diseased kidneys had to be removed, and one would be replaced with an organ from a donor. The operation could not take place, however, until a suitable donor was found. The donor had to be in good health and have blood and body tissue types that were compatible with Lopez's.

Lopez continued to work during this time. He continued to work on *George Lopez,* attend script readings, rehearse, and tape shows. Although Lopez's condition was critical, and he was facing death without a transplant, he knew that more than 150 people were relying on him for jobs. He did not want to let them down by suddenly discontinuing production of his show. He was often tired and in pain as he met production deadlines, but his work onstage let him forget his physical problems for a time. "When you're performing on stage, there's a weightlessness," he said. "You're without pain."[69]

Gift of Life

Fortunately for Lopez, his wife, Ann, was found to have blood and body tissue types that matched her husband's. She did not hesitate to give him her kidney. "There was no question," says Ann. "When you are put in that position where you could possibly lose someone you love, it's a very easy decision."[70]

By the time he underwent transplant surgery in April 2005, Lopez's kidneys had almost stopped working. He was more concerned about his wife than himself, however, and cried when she was taken in for the two-and-a-half-hour operation in which her kidney was removed. Then, in a five-hour operation, the kidney was transferred to Lopez. Both surgeries were successful. The painful, tiring surgery saved Lopez's life. He recovered quickly, and only ten days after surgery he was able to play golf. He finally felt healthy. He improved his diet and lost weight.

Lopez and his wife Ann accept honors at the National Kidney Foundation of Southern California's Gift of Life Celebration in 2006. When Lopez needed a kidney transplant in 2005, Ann donated one of hers to him.

Spreading the Word

Surviving kidney disease inspired Lopez to encourage his audiences, and Latinos in general, to take better care of themselves. In addition to becoming a spokesperson for the National

Lopez used his various appearances, including his television program, to promote issues of health. The show included a storyline about bedwetting by Luis Armand Garcia's character, left, in order to bring attention to the problem and its connection to kidney disease.

Kidney Foundation, he also brought up the topic during his stand-up act and media interviews. In an interview for *WEBMD the Magazine,* he noted, "The people who come to see me do stand-up, they never go to the doctor. I tell them, you need to go! You need to get your blood checked. That can tell you so much."[71]

Lopez also used his television show as a platform to teach people about kidney disease and the importance of proper medical care. During the show's fifth season, an episode was dedicated to examining how George's son, Max, suffered from kidney problems that made him wet the bed. As had happened to Lopez when he was a child, Max's family did not suspect it was a physical problem. "It wasn't hard to do those lines," Lopez said. "My character wouldn't have known or suspected something really was wrong."[72] At the urging of a friend, Lopez eventually takes Max to the doctor and Max gets the care he needs.

Team Lopez

After his kidney transplant, Lopez had a newfound appreciation for his family. He admired his wife for the constant support she had given him, and for saving his life. "She's it, man, she's it," Lopez said in an ABC interview. "And she's been telling me she was it forever and it took me a long time to believe her but she's right." To Ann, giving her kidney to her husband was just another example of the way in which they are a team. "We have worked as a team every step of the way," she once said. "We make every decision together."

George and Ann remained a team even after they divorced in 2010. They continue to be partners in The Lopez Foundation and work together in business.

Quoted in *Primetime*, "Gift of Life from a Comedian's Wife," May 12, 2005. http://abcnews.go.com/Primetime/Health/story?id=752883&page=1.

Ann and George Lopez appear at a golf event sponsored by their foundation in 2010. Despite their divorce, they continue to work together on charitable and business activities.

Movie Maker with Mixed Results

Lopez's health issues did not slow down his career, however. Even before he had the kidney transplant, he fulfilled his commitment to play multiple roles in the family film *The Adventures of Sharkboy & Lavagirl*, a 2005 movie that featured Taylor Lautner and Taylor Dooley as figments of a boy's imagination that become real. Lopez

Lopez walks the red carpet at the premier of Beverly Hills Chihuahua *in 2008 holding its canine star, Rusco. Lopez did the voice work for Rusco's character, Papi, in the film.*

lent charm to his roles, noted reviewer Richard Corliss, even though he criticized the movie overall for having an "amateur atmosphere."[73]

Lopez also teamed up with Ann Lopez in 2009 to make *Mr. Troop Mom*, which she produced. He played the part of Eddie Serrano, a widowed lawyer who goes to summer camp with his daughter in an effort to get to know her better. The movie had a predictable plot, but provided innocent, likable family entertainment.

Lopez also lent his voice to a number of other family movies. In 2008's *Beverly Hills Chihuahua,* he voiced the role of Papi, a Chihuahua trying to rescue the dog he loves. The movie was popular enough to generate a sequel in 2011, and Lopez was part of that film as well. In addition, Lopez signed on to do voice work for *Rio,* a 2011 animated movie about a bird flying to South America. Also in 2011 he was slated to do the voice of Grouchy Smurf in a movie about the little blue cartoon people. In 2010, he was the voice of a house cat in *Marmaduke,* a movie about a dog who moves with his family to Southern California. Unlike *Chihuahua*, the movie was panned, however, for simply not being funny. Lopez had a similar experience with the family-focused action movie *The Spy Next Door* (2010). The movie received horrible reviews, with Lael Lowenstein of *Variety* noting that "the pic's cartoonish jokes and misfired gags are likely to elicit more eye rolls than laughs."[74]

Lopez received mixed reviews in movies that were aimed at adults, too. For example, he was selected to be part of the star-studded cast of *Valentine's Day* in 2010, and shared scenes with Ashton Kutcher. The movie received poor reviews, however; reviewers criticized it for being confusing. Lopez was also part of the disappointing *Henry Poole Is Here* (2008). This film starred Luke Wilson as a man who learns to appreciate life after facing death. As a transplant patient, the film appealed to Lopez because of its hopeful theme. However, reviewers disliked this movie too. Owen Gleiberman of *Entertainment Weekly* wrote that it was "less of a tale of religious rebirth than a faith-based Hallmark card."[75]

Lopez fared better with the critics in the movie *Swing Vote*, which was also released in 2008. He played a television station manager, a role that had been written for a non-Hispanic. This movie was a notable step for Lopez, as it proved that he had transcended the label of being a Latino actor. Kevin Costner starred in the film, about a down-and-out man whose single vote will determine the outcome of a heated presidential election. The movie was criticized for having an improbable plot, but was also praised for the way it captured the political tension that was so prevalent that election year.

An Obama Man

Lopez did not shy away from real-life politics that year either. During the 2008 presidential campaign, Lopez endorsed Barack Obama for president and appeared with him at a debate and several campaign stops. He threw his support behind Obama because he admired Obama's leadership skills and thought Obama's election could both lift Americans' spirits and address the economic

Lopez flashes a Barack Obama t-shirt at a movie premiere in 2008. Lopez's support for Obama during the 2008 campaign included appearances at several political rallies.

downturn. Lopez also believed Obama would bring a new sense of cultural inclusiveness to Washington, D.C. "You'd like to feel like the White House is your house. It belongs to the people," he said, before grinning and adding, "Brown people too."[76]

Since the election, Lopez has maintained a connection to the Obama administration. He was invited to the White House, for example, for an event honoring Mexican president Felipe

Calderón. The May 2010 event featured two hundred guests, including celebrities Beyoncé, Jay-Z, and Eva Longoria Parker.

Obama also did Lopez a favor in his next career venture. He agreed to film a promotional ad for *Lopez Tonight,* a new late-night talk show Lopez began hosting in the fall of 2009. In the ad, Lopez asks Obama if he will consider him for a cabinet position, perhaps ambassador to Mexico. Obama declines, telling George, "You need to change late-night," Obama says. "That's the kind of change I can believe in."[77]

It is unusual for a president to promote a television show, but Lopez had helped Obama during the campaign and the president was grateful for his support. Lopez noted that Obama's campaign helped him shape the spirit of the show, which he intended to be upbeat and multicultural. "I was inspired by campaigning with Barack Obama and that message of inclusiveness and diversity,"

The Latino Vote

George Lopez's support for Barack Obama in the 2008 campaign was especially significant because of the important role the Hispanic vote played in the election. There were large Hispanic populations in states that could swing the election toward either Obama or his opponent, John McCain, and both Republicans and Democrats were hoping to convince Hispanics to vote for them. Latino voters understood the importance of casting a ballot. In the 2008 Presidential election, the number of Latinos who voted increased by 25 percent over 2004.

Two-thirds of America's Hispanics voted for Obama, which helped secure him the presidency. "They really delivered," said Efrain Escobedo, who was part of a group that encouraged Latinos to register to vote. "This is an electorate [group of voters] that now understands the importance of voting, and they made a significant shift in the political landscape."

Quoted in Julia Preston, "In Big Shift, Latino Vote Was Heavily for Obama," *New York Times,* November 7, 2008. www.nytimes.com/2008/11/07/us/politics/07latino.html.

he said in an interview in *People* magazine. "It's time for that change to come to TV."[78]

A New Voice in Talk Shows

Lopez hoped *Lopez Tonight* would have the same energy as the show Arsenio Hall had hosted in the early 1990s. The forty-eight-year-old host planned to include guests from a variety of ethnic backgrounds and present a street-party atmosphere. Obama's endorsement gave him a significant boost in visibility, but the entertainer still faced challenges. For one, his show was on TBS rather than a broadcast network; in addition to the likelihood that the cable channel would draw fewer viewers than the major networks, talk shows were a new venture for TBS.

When the show premiered in November 2009, some wondered if it was really as groundbreaking as Lopez had promised it would be. Reviewer Mike Hale pointed out that Lopez proclaimed, "The

Actor Samuel L. Jackson, left, is interviewed by Lopez on the set of his talk show, Lopez Tonight, *which debuted on TBS in 2009.*

revolution starts now!"[79] in his first show, but Hale failed to see how it was different from any other talk show. "After watching the program's first week, it was hard to see what exactly the revolution consisted of," he said, noting that the only difference he saw was some crude humor. "Otherwise, 'Lopez Tonight' was business as usual: a comedian on an ugly set telling jokes and making fawning chit-chat with celebrities."[80]

While the show received initial criticism, it did pull in viewers. It attracted an initial audience of almost 1 million people, and as the weeks went on Lopez began drawing the youngest audience of any late-night host. In addition, Lopez became the first Latino to host a late-night talk show, a milestone for him and for television.

Lopez barely had time settle into his new role before he was brought into a talk-show controversy, however. A shakeup at NBC involved Lopez soon after his show debuted. Jay Leno had hosted *The Tonight Show* since the early 1990s, but left that program in September 2009 to host a new program, *The Jay Leno Show*, in an earlier time slot. This show, however, failed to attract a large audience, and Leno was asked to return to *The Tonight Show*, which was now hosted by comedian Conan O'Brien. NBC offered O'Brien a later time slot for his show, but he refused. He was not without a show for long, however. TBS offered O'Brien the chance to host a late-night show on that cable network, which meant that Lopez's show would be bumped to one hour later. This could potentially cost him a good share of his audience, since television viewership in general drops later in the evening.

Lopez agreed to the switch, however. Bringing O'Brien on board helped secure his show for another season and also gave him a strong lead-in program for his show, which he thought might actually help him attract more viewers. Calling their programs "Team Loco," a combination of his last name and O'Brien's first, Lopez noted, "I think it's going to be a compelling block of television. He's going to help me."[81] After more than twenty years in the entertainment business, Lopez had learned that success involved some give and take. He might not have the prime time slot, but he knew what could help his show in the long run.

Humoring People

The format of *Lopez Tonight* was similar to that of other late-night talk shows, with a monologue and celebrity interviews. Veteran comedian Bill Cosby, teen actress Selena Gomez, award-winning actor and director Clint Eastwood, wrestler Mike "The Miz" Mizanin, and rapper Sean Combs all appeared on the show. Musical guests ranged from rocker Ted Nugent to the Chicano band Los Lobos. Lopez tried to set his show apart, however, by getting guests to do quirky things. For example, he ate deep-fried bacon with comedian Will Farrell and got actor Zac Efron to taste bugs. He also visited the homes of singer Marc Antony and actor Jamie Foxx.

Even as he ventured into new territory, however, Lopez did not give up on the stand-up comedy that had set his career in motion. He continued to go on the road and aimed to pull in bigger and bigger crowds. "I don't think you ever really fully develop as a comedian—much like if you were a runner, you would always challenge yourself,"[82] he says.

Lopez has continued to make strides with his career and enjoy his work, but his personal life took a new turn in 2010. Shortly after his seventeenth wedding anniversary, he and Ann announced they were divorcing. They both agreed that ending their marriage was the right thing for them to do, although they continued to do business together and work together with the Lopez Foundation.

Lopez's work with the foundation and his groundbreaking television shows were among the impressive gains he had made over the course of his career. In taking the humor, pride, and pain of his background and Mexican American heritage to the stage, Lopez had become an influential figure who brought humor to his audience and pride to his culture.

Introduction: Laughing Through Pain

1. Quoted in Mireya Navarro, "A Life So Sad He Had to Be Funny," *New York Times,* November 27, 2002. www.nytimes.com/ 2002/11/27/arts/life-so-sad-he-had-be-funny-george-lopez- mines-rich-vein-gloom-with-all-latino.html?pagewanted=all.
2. Quoted in Oprah.com, "Q&A with George Lopez," November 9, 2009. www.oprah.com/oprahshow/George-Lopezs-New- Talk-Show.
3. Quoted in Oprah.com, "Q&A with George Lopez."

Chapter 1: Growing Pains

4. George Lopez with Armen Keteyian, *Why You Crying? My Long Hard Look at Life, Love, and Laughter.* New York: Touchstone, 2004, p. 18.
5. Lopez with Keteyian, *Why You Crying?*, p. 34.
6. Quoted in *Primetime*, "Gift of Life from a Comedian's Wife," ABC News, May 12, 2005. http://abcnews.go.com/Primetime/ Health/story?id=752883&page=1.
7. Quoted in Navarro, "A Life So Sad He Had to Be Funny."
8. Quoted in Robert Deitsch et al., "George Lopez," *Sports Illustrated*, September 5, 2005, p. 28.
9. Lopez with Keteyian, *Why You Crying?*, p. 17.

Chapter 2: Comic Commitment

10. Quoted in Cynthia Wang, "George Lopez," *People*, September 5, 2003. www.people.com/people/article/0,,628313,00.html.
11. Quoted in Eric Deggans, "By George!" *Hispanic,* September 2003, p. 46.
12. Lopez with Keteyian, *Why You Crying?*, p. 55.
13. Quoted in Katy Vine, "George Lopez," *Texas Monthly*, July 2004, p. 30.
14. Quoted in Wang, "George Lopez."

15. Quoted in *Lopez Tonight,* "George in His Own Words, Part 4: Arsenio," October 15, 2009. www.lopeztonight.com/ george_in_his_own_words/george_in_his_own_words_arsenio. php.

16. Quoted in *Lopez Tonight,* "George in His Own Words, Part 4: Arsenio."

17. Rita Kempley, "Ski Patrol," *Washington Post,* January 13, 1990. www.washingtonpost.com/wp-srv/style/longterm/movies/ videos/skipatrolpg13kempley_a0c995.htm.

18. George Lopez, *Latino Kings of Comedy, Volume 2.* DVD. Lionsgate Entertainment, 1982–1995.

19. Lopez, *Latino Kings of Comedy, Volume 2.*

Chapter 3: Finding the Right Stuff

20. Lopez with Keteyian, *Why You Crying?,* p. 82.

21. Quoted in Stacy Wilson, "Fifty Latino … ," *Variety,* March 9, 2006, p. A8.

22. Quoted in Deggans, "By George!" p. 46.

23. Lopez with Keteyian, *Why You Crying?,* p. 84.

24. Quoted in *Primetime,* "Gift of Life from a Comedian's Wife."

25. Quoted in Oprah.com, "Q&A with George Lopez."

26. George Lopez, *The Original Latin Kings of Comedy.* DVD. Paramount Pictures, 2002.

27. Lopez, *The Original Latin Kings of Comedy.*

28. Lopez with Keteyian, *Why You Crying?,* p. 16.

29. Quoted in James Poniewozik, "The Prime-Time Funny Man," *Time,* August 22, 2005, p. 45.

30. Quoted in Marissa Rodriguez, "George's Way," *Hispanic,* August 2008, p. 52.

31. Roger Ebert, "Bread and Roses," *Chicago Sun-Times,* June 1, 2001. http://rogerebert.suntimes.com/apps/pbcs.dll/ article?AID=/20010601/REVIEWS/106010301.

32. Lisa Schwarzbaum, "Real Women Have Curves," *Entertainment Weekly,* October 23, 2002. www.ew.com/ew/ article/0,,380734,00.html.

33. Quoted in James Poniewozik and Jeanne McDowell, "Prime-Time Therapy," *Time,* March 24, 2003, p. 64.

34. Quoted in Deggans, "By George!" p. 46.
35. Quoted in Michael Schneider, "Latinos Get Leverage," *Variety,* June 30, 2003, p. 17.
36. Quoted in Schneider, "Latinos Get Leverage," p. 17.
37. Stephen M. Silverman, "ABC's 'George Lopez' May Be New Hit," *People,* April 3, 2002. www.people.com/people/article/0,,623856,00.html.
38. *George Lopez: The Complete First and Second Seasons,* "Episode 1: Prototype." DVD. Warner Home Video, April 17, 2007.
39. *George Lopez: The Complete First and Second Seasons,* "Episode 1: Prototype." DVD. Warner Home Video, April 17, 2007.
40. L. Brent Bozell III, "Is Hollywood Finally Tuning Back In to American Dream?" *Insight on the News,* November 12, 2002, p. 51.
41. Quoted in Deggans, "By George!" p. 46.
42. Navarro, "A Life So Sad He Had to Be Funny."
43. John Markert, "The George Lopez Show: The Same Old Hispano?" *Bilingual Review,* January 1, 1007, p. 160.
44. Quoted in Al Carlos Hernandez, "Ann Serrano Lopez—Wife, Mother, Media Mogul," *La Prensa San Diego,* January 22, 2010, p. 4.
45. Ross Dalton, "Stand-Up Guys," *Entertainment Weekly,* February 27, 2004, p. 84.
46. Quoted in Wang, "George Lopez."
47. Robert Bianco, "Critic's Corner," *USA Today,* January 24, 2007, p. 8D.
48. Quoted in Maria Elena Fernandez, "TV Just Got a Lot 'Whiter,' Says a Canceled George Lopez," *Los Angeles Times,* May 14, 2007. http://latimesblogs.latimes.com/showtracker/2007/05/post_1.html.
49. Quoted in Fernandez, "TV Just Got a Lot 'Whiter,' Says a Canceled George Lopez."
50. Quoted in Paige Albiniak, "Lopez a Sleeper Hit," *Broadcasting and Cable,* April 13, 2008. www.broadcastingcable.com/article/113266-Lopez_A_Sleeper_Hit.php.
51. Quoted in Rodriguez, "George's Way," p. 52.

52. Quoted in Brett Wilbur, "Non-Stop Lopez Gets Big Laughs While Tackling Heavy Topics," *Carmel*, Winter 2007. www.carmelmagazine.com/archive/07wi/george-lopez.shtml.

53. George Lopez, interview by Tavis Smiley, *Tavis Smiley: Late Night on PBS*, KCET-PBS, August 13, 2008. www.pbs.org/kcet/tavissmiley/archive/200808/20080813_lopez.html.

54. Quoted in Lopez with Keteyian, *Why You Crying?*, p. 158.

55. Pete Allman, "George Lopez Rocks a Full House at the Las Vegas Hilton," October 27, 2009, News Blaze.com. http://newsblaze.com/story/20091027122705allm.nb/topstory.html.

56. Quoted in Lorenza Muñoz, "George Lopez on Comedy and Race," *Smithsonian*, August 2010. www.smithsonianmag.com/specialsections/40th-anniversary/George-Lopez-on-Comedy-and-Race.html.

57. Quoted in Muñoz, "George Lopez on Comedy and Race."

58. John Doyle, "Laughs, Mystery and Big, Toothy Critters—Yes, It's Shark Week," *Globe and Mail*, July 31, 2010. www.theglobeandmail.com/news/arts/television/john-doyle/laughs-mystery-and-big-toothy-critters-yes-its-shark-week/article1657288/.

59. Quoted in Scott Gummer, "Looping for Lopez," *Golf*, July 2004, p. 43.

60. Quoted in Gummer, "Looping for Lopez," p. 43.

61. Quoted in Bob Verdi, "A Latino with a Club—and a Gift," *Golf World*, January 27, 2007, p. 52.

62. Quoted in Jamie Diaz, "G-Lo," *Golf Digest*, February 2008, p. 104.

63. George Lopez, "Pebble Beach Scene Brings My Golf Journey Full Circle," *Sports Illustrated*, February 8, 2007. http://sportsillustrated.cnn.com/vault/article/web/COM1058252/index.htm.

64. George Lopez, interview by Tavis Smiley.

65. Quoted in Hernandez, "Ann Serrano Lopez—Wife, Mother, Media Mogul," p. 4.

66. Robert Mitchell, "Award Winning Actor, Comedian George Lopez Named the 2004 Artist of the Year at Harvard," *Harvard University Faculty of Arts and Sciences, News and*

Notices, February 24, 2004. www.fas.harvard.edu/home/news-and-notices/news/press-releases/release-archive/releases-2004/lopez-02242004.shtml.

67. Quoted in Poniewozik, "The Prime-Time Funny Man," p. 45.

Chapter 6: No Backing Down

68. Quoted in Matt McMillen, "George Lopez Finds a Perfect Match," WebMD the Magazine. http://men.webmd.com/features/perfect-match.
69. Quoted in McMillen, "George Lopez Finds a Perfect Match."
70. Quoted in *Primetime*, "Gift of Life from a Comedian's Wife."
71. Quoted in McMillen, "George Lopez Finds a Perfect Match."
72. Quoted in McMillen, "George Lopez Finds a Perfect Match."
73. Richard Corliss, "For Children of All Ages," *Time*, June 13, 2005, p. 53.
74. Lael Loewenstein, "The Spy Next Door," *Variety*, January 9, 2010. www.variety.com/review/VE1117941861.html?categoryid=31&cs=1.
75. Owen Gleiberman, "Henry Poole Is Here," *Entertainment Weekly*, August 15, 2008. www.ew.com/ew/article/0,,20219196,00.html.
76. Quoted in Juan Castillo, "George Lopez Plays the Spin Room," *Austin American-Statesman,* February 21, 2008. www.statesman.com/blogs/content/shared-gen/blogs/austin/politics/entries/2008/02/21/george_lopez_plays_the_spin_ro.html.
77. Quoted in TBS, "Lopez Tonight," trailer. www.youtube.com/watch?v=VflFOiwCflM.
78. Quoted in Blaine Zuckerman, "Working the Late Shift," *People*, November 16, 2009, p. 43.
79. Quoted in Mike Hale, "Late-Night Revolution: In Taste, Perhaps," *New York Times,* November 14, 2009, p. C1.
80. Hale, "Late-Night Revolution," p. C1.
81. Quoted in *Los Angeles Times*, "Lopez on Late Night with Conan, Golf and, Yes, 'The Smurfs,'" April 21, 2010. http://latimesblogs.latimes.com/gossip/2010/04/george-lopez-late-night-conan-golf-smurfs.html.
82. Quoted in Oprah.com, "Q&A with George Lopez."

Important Dates

1961

George Lopez is born in East Los Angeles on April 23.

1979

Lopez becomes the first person in his extended family to graduate from high school. He performs his first stand-up routine on graduation night.

1980

A frustrated Lopez leaves stand-up comedy.

1982

Lopez returns to the comedy stage and begins to perform consistently.

1987

Lopez leaves his day job and becomes a full-time comedian.

1989

Lopez makes his first of sixteen appearances on *The Arsenio Hall Show.*

1993

Lopez's marries Ann Serrano on September 18.

1995

Ann and George's daughter, Mayan, is born.

2000

A recording of his stand-up act is released on the *Alien Nation* CD. Lopez returns to movies with a part in *Bread and Roses.*

2002

George Lopez premieres on national television. Lopez also releases the CD *Team Leader*, which is nominated for a Grammy Award.

2004

A kidney ailment causes Lopez severe pain, and he learns he needs a kidney transplant. He receives a kidney transplant the following year with his wife as the donor.

2005

Time magazine names Lopez one of the "25 Most Influential Hispanics in America."

2007

George Lopez is cancelled. Lopez appears in the movies *Balls of Fury* and *Tortilla Heaven*.

2009

Lopez's late-night talk show *Lopez Tonight* debuts on TBS. Lopez's performance in San Antonio, Texas, is recorded for the television special *Tall, Dark, and Chicano*.

2010

Lopez's movie work in includes *Valentine's Day, The Spy Next Door*, and *Marmaduke*.
Lopez and his wife, Ann, divorce after seventeen years of marriage.

For More Information

Books

Lila Guzman and Rick Guzman, *George Lopez: Latino King of Comedy*. Berkeley Heights, NJ: Enslow, 2008. The story of Lopez's childhood and rise to fame.

George Lopez with Armen Keteyian, *Why You Crying?* New York: Touchstone, 2004. Lopez takes a frank look at his childhood years, his start in standup comedy, and the first years of his television sitcom.

DVDs

George Lopez the Complete First and Second Seasons. 2002. This DVD set includes episodes from Lopez's television show, as well as an interview with the actor.

Brown Is the New Green: George Lopez and the American Dream. 2007. This documentary by Philip Rodriguez looks at Lopez's career and the impact Hispanics make on the U.S. economy.

Periodicals

Eric Deggans, "By George!" *Hispanic,* September 2003.

Scott Gummer, "Looping for Lopez," *Golf,* July 2004.

Mireya Navarro, "A Life So Sad He Had to Be Funny," *New York Times,* November 27, 2002.

Marissa Rodriguez, "George's Way," *Hispanic,* August 2008.

Internet Sources

Natalie Finn, "George Lopez Is Already LoCo for CoCo," April 12, 2010. www.eonline.com/uberblog/b176113_george_lopez_already_loco_coco.html.

Louise Fenner, "Hispanics, the Largest U.S. Minority, Enrich the American Mosaic," America.gov, September 22, 2009. www.america.gov/st/peopleplace-english/2009/September/20090921163442xlrennef0.8085836.html.

Tavis Smiley, "George Lopez," *Tavis Smiley,* August 13, 2008, http://www.pbs.org/kcet/tavissmiley/archive/200808/20080813_lopez.html.

Websites

The Ann and George Lopez Foundation (www.thelopez-foundation.org). The official site of the Ann & George Lopez Foundation includes information about the organization, its fund-raising events, and board members.

George Lopez (www.georgelopez.com). Lopez's official site includes a biography of the star, tour dates, and news updates. It also includes information about his foundation and games for kids.

Lopez Tonight (www.lopeztonight.com). This site offers videos from Lopez's television show, information about how to get tickets to see it, and behind-the scenes information about his new movies.

M
Marriage, 43, 81, *81*
Movies
  acting roles, 36–37
  The Adventures of Sharkboy &
    Lavagirl, 81–82
  Bread and Roses, 45
  Mr. Troop Mom, 82
  The Original Latin Kings of
    Comedy, 62, 64
  Real Women Have Curves, 45
  reviews, 83
  Ski Patrol, 32, 34
  voice acting, 82–83
Mr. Troop Mom (movie), 82

N
Nickelodeon, 59

O
Obama, Barack, 83–85
O'Brien, Conan, 87
The Original Latin Kings of
  Comedy (movie), 62, 64

P
Parents, 12–14
Pebble Beach golf course, *69*, 70
Personal life
  divorce, 81, 88
  golf, 69–71, *69*, *71*
  marriage, 43, *81*
  self-destructive habits, 37–38
Politics, 83–86, *84*
Prinze, Freddie, *19*, 20, 22–23
Pryor, Richard, 22, 23

R
Radio, 44–45
Real Women Have Curves
  (movie), 45

Recordings, 44, 67, 69
Reviews, 45, 83
Role modeling, 11, 71–72, 75
Role models, *19*, 20–23

S
Serrano, Ann. *See Lopez, Ann*
Ski Patrol (movie), 32, *34*
Stage presence, 24–26
Stereotypes, 9, 36–37, 54–56,
  63, 64, 66, 70
Swing Vote (movie), 83
Syndication of *George Lopez*
  (television show), 59, 61

T
Talk shows, 85, 86–88
TBS television network,
  86, 87
Television
  Arsenio Hall Show
    appearance, 32
  awards shows, 67
  Bullock, Sandra, offer by,
    46–47
  childhood love of, 19–20
  Dancing with the Stars, 74
  Lopez Tonight, 85, 86–88
  stand-up comedy show
    appearances, 34
  See also George Lopez
    (television show)
Transplant, kidney,
  77–79
Trevino, Lee, 21, *21*, 70–71

V
Voice acting, 82–83

W
Wedding, 43

About the Author

Terri Dougherty is the author of more than eighty books for children. She lives in Appleton, Wisconsin, with her husband, Denis, and their three children, Kyle, Rachel, and Emily. She enjoys traveling with her family, as well as playing soccer, jogging, and skiing. George Lopez can always make her laugh.